D0085642

400

9

also by Perry Meisel

The Myth of the Modern
A Study in British Literature and Criticism after 1850

Bloomsbury/Freud
The Letters of James and Alix Strachey, 1924–25 (Co-ed.)

Freud
A Collection of Critical Essays (Ed.)

The Absent Father
Virginia Woolf and Walter Pater

Thomas Hardy
The Return of the Repressed

the COWBOY and the *Dandy*

the
COWBOY
and the *Dandy*

Crossing Over from

Romanticism to

Rock and Roll

Perry Meisel

New York   Oxford

Oxford University Press

1999

Oxford University Press

Oxford   New York
Athens   Auckland   Bangkok   Bogotá   Buenos Aires   Calcutta
Cape Town   Chennai   Dar es Salaam   Delhi   Florence   Hong Kong   Istanbul
Karachi   Kuala Lumpur   Madrid   Melbourne   Mexico City   Mumbai
Nairobi   Paris   São Paulo   Singapore   Tokyo   Toronto   Warsaw

and associated companies in
Berlin   Ibadan

Copyright © 1999 by Perry Meisel

Published by Oxford University Press, Inc.
198 Madison Avenue, New York, New York 10016

Oxford is a registered trademark of Oxford University Press

All rights reserved. No part of this publication may be reproduced,
stored in a retrieval system, or transmitted, in any form or by any means,
electronic, mechanical, photocopying, recording, or otherwise,
without the prior permission of Oxford University Press.

Library of Congress Cataloging-in-Publication Data
Meisel, Perry.
The cowboy and the dandy : crossing over from Romanticism to rock
and roll / by Perry Meisel.
p.   cm.
Includes bibliographical references and index.
ISBN 0-19-511817-0
1. Music and literature.   2. Rock music—United States—History
and criticism.   I. Title.
ML3849.M49   1998
700'.973—dc21   97-23789

9 8 7 6 5 4 3 2 1

Printed in the United States of America
on acid-free paper

ACKNOWLEDGMENTS

Publication of this book has been aided by a grant from the Abraham and Rebecca Stein Faculty Publication Fund of New York University, Department of English. Grateful acknowledgment is made to Special Rider Music for permission to reprint lyrics from Bob Dylan's "My Back Pages" (copyright 1964 by Warner Bros. Music, copyright renewed 1992 by Special Rider Music) and "Love Minus Zero" (copyright 1965 by Warner Bros. Music, copyright renewed 1993 by Special Rider Music). All rights reserved. International copyright secured. Reprinted by permission.

Thanks to all who provided guidance during the preparation of *The Cowboy and the Dandy,* particularly Harold Bloom, Robert Christgau, Gary Giddins, Mary Lawlor, and Nick Smart. Thanks also to Toby Greenberg for photoresearch. A portion of chapter 8, on Virginia Woolf's *Orlando,* originally appeared in *Deconstruction is/in America,* ed. Anselm Haverkamp (New York: New York University Press, 1995). Portions of chapter 9, on Led Zeppelin and the Ramones, first appeared in *The Village Voice* in somewhat different form.

CONTENTS

a NOTE on CITATION

A systematic form of citation has been employed throughout. Whether literary or musical, all works cited are followed by the writer's or musician's name (unless given in the text) and a date. In the case of written works, page numbers may also accompany the date; in the case of musical works, the date indicates date of recording release. A list of works cited appears at the back, divided into a bibliography and a discography. Songwriters are included in a discographical listing only if they are different from the performer or performers given in the text.

the COWBOY and the *Dandy*

The various forms of intellectual activity which together make up the culture of an age, move for the most part from different starting-points, and by unconnected roads. As products of the same generation they partake indeed of a common character, and unconsciously illustrate each other.

—Walter Pater, Preface to *Studies in the History of the Renaissance* (1873)

A whale ship was my Yale College and my Harvard.
—Herman Melville,
Moby-Dick (1851)

How do we know who copied what?
—Louis Armstrong (1960)

INTRODUCTION

Crossing Over

On April 13, 1882, Oscar Wilde, dressed in a green over-coat and black slouch hat, climbed into a large bucket and was lowered down a mine shaft in Leadville, Colorado. Wilde was on the Western swing of an American lecture tour that had begun in New York some four months earlier. As Richard Ellmann tells us in his biography, Wilde was more impressed with the miners and the cowboys than he was with much of the company he had been forced to endure earlier in his trip. "They were polished and refined compared with the people I met in larger cities farther East," said Wilde. "There is no chance for roughness. The revolver," he drawled, "is their book of etiquette" (1988, 204). At the bottom of the mine, high and deep in the Rocky Mountains, Wilde discovered that two ceremonies had been prepared in his honor. The first involved drinking whiskey for dinner. The second required him to use a drill to open a new shaft in the mine, a shaft that the Silver King, Leadville's mayor, R. A. W. Tabor, had named "The Oscar" as a proleptic Hollywood tribute to the aesthetic visitor from England. Afterward, the assembled company went off to a casino, where there was music. Wilde recalled the scene in some detail:

> There I found the miners and the female friends of the miners, and in one corner a pianist—sitting at a piano over which was this notice: "Please don't shoot the pianist; he is doing his best." I was struck with this recognition of the fact that bad art merits the penalty of death, and I felt that in this remote city, where the aesthetic applications of the revolver were clearly established in the case of

3

music, my apostolic task would be much simplified, as indeed it was. (1988, 204)

This was the Wilde West.

Such an unlikely affection between the most famous dandy of the day and a bunch of rugged Westerners is unsettling. After all, the nineteenth century supposedly produced two very different kinds of drama on each side of the Atlantic. In America, Westward expansion dominated Romantic imagination. In England and on the Continent, inward expansion dominated, as bohemianism followed Romanticism, aestheticism followed bohemianism, and modernism was heir to them all. To the customary notion that American expansionism had little to do with the East or with Europe—a wish-fulfillment in its own right, as we shall see—the reply is that New York's skyscrapers, complete with their canyon effects, were built, however unconsciously, in the belated image of the West. Frederick Jackson Turner declared the frontier closed in 1893; Manhattan's mesa-like Flatiron Building was erected in 1902 (the far grander Metropolitan Life Building rose in 1909 and the Woolworth Building in 1913), even though the hydraulic elevator had been experimentally perfected by George H. Fox & Company as early as 1850, and some high-rise structures had begun to appear in other American cities, notably Chicago, in the 1880s and 1890s (see also Douglas 1995, 436; see Curtis 1982, 40). A reciprocity attends the presumably unrelated cultural histories of nineteenth-century America and nineteenth-century England. As different as they may seem to be, these twins of High Romanticism—American expansion and aesthetic inwardness—are versions of one another and tell an uncannily similar story as the century unfolds.

But what about the piano player? Black or white, he—or she—was surely playing African-American music, the music that by 1882 had already begun to overwhelm the square sound of the European music hall still featured in New York saloons and give it a jelly roll appropriate to the swagger of cowboy and dandy alike. Of course, in 1882, the music in the Colorado casino was probably a precursor of ragtime, a hybrid of the European and the African, but it might just as likely have been an early form of boogie-woogie piano, a tougher blues style that was sometimes called "Western" piano, as LeRoi Jones observed in 1963, "meaning that the music had originated in the mining and lumber camps of the West and Midwest" (114). Ragtime would in any case go on to play a part in the transformation of country blues early in the twentieth century into the classic blues of Ma Rainey and Louis Armstrong, the tradition that leads directly to both jazz and rock and roll—Duke Ellington's first composition at age fourteen was entitled "Soda Fountain Rag" (1913)—and that rehearses in its particular way a story not unlike the cowboy and the dandy's own. In each case a drama is just beginning that, by the late 1950s, less than a century after Wilde and the cowboys boogie woogie, manifestly joins African-American and Romantic culture and leads, with some irony, to the construction of a transatlantic, even global culture in its own right. The "electric influence" (1882a, 10:33) that Wilde notes among Americans may look back to Whitman for the metaphor, but it looks ahead to rock and roll for its literalization and institutional fulfillment.

WHY AND HOW DID Anglo-America and Afro-America find a common ground in rock and roll? What in each tradition's history predetermined this decisive relation? What links Romanticism and blues tradition? The answer is simple. What links cowboy and dandy is the Romantic preoccupation with boundaries. It is also what links them both with the culture of Afro-America. If cowboy and dandy are the extreme nineteenth-century devolutions in America and England, respectively, of the High Romantic paradoxes of circumscribed strength and ironic freedom—Shelley's Prometheus comes to mind, or Byron's Cain—they have an exact counterpart in the preoccupation with boundaries in African-American culture, particularly the boundary or dialectic between country and city that structures black American imagination in the twentieth century. From World War I to 1970, millions of black Americans moved from South to North, much as, throughout the nineteenth and twentieth centuries, millions of white Americans moved from East to West. Two geographies of mind replace two geographies of place. Country and city, cowboy and dandy, are, structurally, mirror images of one another and behave in strikingly similar ways. Each is a paradigm that redoubles the others in a different categorical key: for the cowboy, the boundary or opposition between East and West, settlement and frontier; for the dandy, the boundary or opposition between self and world, inside and outside; for country and city, the boundary or opposition between North and South, urban and folk.

When cowboy and dandy come together overtly, as they eventually do in the fashion and iconography of Romantic culture by the 1960s, they produce the fluidity of relation between urban and outdoor that we readily associate with white or Romantic rock culture and rock music each alike. The combination of cowboy and dandy is everywhere: blue jeans and blazers, lipstick and leather, flannel shirts and electric guitars. The early Bob Dylan mixes bluegrass picking with modernist lyric; the later Elvis Presley mixes country carriage with silky dress. Even the names of bands recapitulate the blend: Guns 'N Roses, Pink Floyd, the Sex Pistols, Iron Butterfly.

But rock and roll is, in its origins and historically, at least until the 1950s, a decidedly African-American affair that, like jazz, goes on to become culturally hegemonic (see also Hamm 1979). Rock and roll is not simply the tight line from Chuck Berry, say, or Buddy Holly to the Beatles, the Byrds, and Nirvana, but also the bigger sound behind it in the larger history of blues tradition (I use the term in its musical sense) that swerves from jazz history proper beginnning with rhythm and blues and electric blues in the 1940s. The fluidity of relation between inside and outside, urban and frontier, cowboy and dandy in later rock and roll is already prefigured by a key like development in the earlier history of African-American culture, and one for which jazz itself is the overriding sign: the invention of a black urbanity (for the term, see Baker 1993, 28) designed to resolve or accommodate the split or difference between country and city itself. Black urbanity is a mode of compensatory imagination not unlike Romanticism's own, and a paradigm far more appropriate to black American experience than the typological one it surpasses.

Of course, when one hears about models for white culture in black, one anticipates the usual Beat or faux Romantic image of the brute primitive. Hence the antithetical power of black urbanity. It provides a model for the situation of black culture and black imagination that rebuts and refashions the fearful image of the savage popular in dominant culture since Exploration days (for a catalog, see Pattison 1987). Black culture is actually just the reverse: the site of a learnedness whose strength derives from its ability to put country and city, frontier and urban, cowboy and dandy into a relation only implicit in a dominant culture whose cowboys and dandies don't combine into a single cultural style until the 1960s. Late in my argument I take the British Invasion of 1964–66 as the conclusive moment for this kind of development—its first consciousness, as it were—and the undoing of a necessity that segregationist America was still trying to repress. Recall that the Civil Rights Act and the Beatles' back-to-back appearances on *The Ed Sullivan Show* both took place in 1964. Here our two histories intersect at a moment decisive for both traditions. Rock and roll provides both Romantic and blues traditions a pivot or hinge of intersection by means of which each finds itself by virtue of finding a relation with the other. Each tradition is a response to loss, and each contains a new formula for imaginative gain; each needs to overcome the disappointments of the quest romance of freedom, and to do so each reimagines the terms with which it begins. The mutuality is startling and has gone too long unexamined.

My intent in the pages that follow, however, is not so much to argue for causality or to demonstrate by way of social history or the study of ideological practices the manner in which cowboy and dandy, Romanticism and blues tradition engage and refigure one another to sustain rock and roll in anything more than a paradigmatic way. Rock and roll is first and foremost a kind of blues music. What its relation may be to a poetic form of imagination such as Romanticism must lie in an aesthetic dimension, and not one confined to the obvious similarities between rock and Romantic lyric alone. This book, then, is really an attempt to provide a frame within which to organize a way to talk about what Romantic and blues traditions share by addressing another difficulty—a methodological one—equally central to the question of the relation between them: the problem of how to talk about literary and musical traditions (and literary and musical texts) in the same breath. What do two discourses about boundaries also share? A rhetoric of boundaries that doubles and supports a rhetoric about them. Here our themes emerge in our forms and our forms in our themes.

Romantic literary language and blues music also share the same characteristic rhetorical figure or movement, what Kenneth Burke, in 1938, well before deconstruction, identified as the rhetorical figure of chiasmus, or crossing over—a loop, as it were—and the master trope that writing and music have in common (1938, 372). I employ the term "crossover" not, however, the way the music business has in the last twenty years—as a kind of dull "fusion," as the saying goes, of maladapted jazz solos over a rock or funky beat—but, following Burke, as rhetoricians do. Chiasmus is a "pattern of mirror inversion," as Richard Lanham describes it, "a natural internal dynamic" in a figure of language—or a figure of music—in which "the second element" wants "to flip over and back over the first" (1991, 33). This figure is, of course, a principle in African music that is familiar in the countrapuntal riffs and rhythms of the blues; it is also the legendary crossroads of the African trickster god Legba. Its linguistic form creates boundaries and parcels out divides simply by being used. If Romanticism, for example, describes mind by means of landscape—Wordsworth's "Tintern Abbey" is a case in point—it also describes landscape by means of mind. Here a connection between mind and world is established by virtue of drawing a distinction between them. We can also use crossing over to describe its musical equivalent and give two examples of how it works at the same time: if Louis Armstrong's horn sounds like a voice, his voice also sounds like a horn. Crossing over is the figure that Romantic and blues languages share.

But, you will say, you read rock and roll through the lens of Romanticism. Of course I do. But I also read Romanticism through the lens of rock and roll, the one as inevitably as the other. That is the problem, but it is also the point, and it is another example of crossing over. Orientalism is, as we all know, a problem with which any cross- or multicultural account is necessarily confronted (Said 1978). Bias or position is a difficulty with which any utterance is enablingly confounded (Fish 1989). The solution is a surprisingly plain one: Orientalism, or "othering," works both ways at once. Everyone's—including one's own—point of view is always contaminated by another's. "Othering," writes Henry Louis Gates, Jr., "starts in the home"; "identities are always in dialogue" (1993, 6, 11). Crossing over turns out to be not just the structure of our subjects, but also of our own perspective as a culture, a "stereophonic" perspective, to borrow Paul Gilroy's term (1993, 3). What methodological difficulties may emerge over the course of our discussion—I shall be attentive to them—are themselves functions of the sites of description in question. What the relation between cowboy and dandy and country and city may be is not a simple or objective one.

To what extent is black urbanity a composite of cowboy and dandy *avant la lettre, avant garde?* To what extent are country and city wholly unrelated to Romantic mythology? To what extent is any formulation of such a relation doomed always to the solemn measure of colonialism and resistance? The structure of our questions and of their objects is as a rule the same. Here is Samuel Charters writing about an African tribal performance in 1981:

> What was I seeing? Where had I seen it before? It was in New Orleans, on a Mardi Gras morning in the early 1950s. What I saw . . . was this same procession of a spirit figure, only in New Orleans the spirit had become an "Indian," through all the confusions of the new culture and the new religion. His costume was an exuberant exaggeration of something that might have been worn for one of Buffalo Bill's Wild West Shows. (1981, 68)

What is the yield of these ironies? Not only the familiar one that no single position is privileged, but also the less familiar one that we are thereby freed from the presumption that any position is particularly natural. This is the book's additional focus—not just to show how country and city, cowboy and dandy are both preoccupied with boundaries and how both structure boundaries in the same way, but also to show that both Romanticism and blues tradition question and expunge the very terms for which they are famous, undoing the difference between nature and culture, influence and originality in the act of asserting it. Much as Ma Rainey belatedly discovers the blues itself from the perspective of vaudeville in 1902 (Palmer 1981, 44), so the crossing from country to city retroactively situates the Southern past within time, culture, and history. It reduces its natural size and subordinates it, the way a rancher does the Western landscape or a dandy does the whole institution of authority. The natural, the country, the cowboy are belatedly discovered, surprised by culture, the city, the dandy. Afro-America redacts American Romanticism's movement, or presumable movement, from East to West—the presumable movement of freedom itself—and shows that freedom, nature, imagination are actually the reverse of what they are customarily assumed to be. For Romantic America, Afro-America "brings," as the Band puts it on Bob Dylan's "I Shall Be Released," "the West back to the East" (1968). In Romantic rock and roll, the West turns back East to acknowledge its influences and its burdens (a theme I shall press in my reading of the mythos of the American West in particular), especially the ironic burden of the Romantic injunction to move beyond culture. In Romantic rock and roll, American expansion is a Wildean sham grounded not in freedom but in a flight from influence.

The shared preoccupation with boundaries in both Romantic and African-American culture leads us to something else we can now see that they share: the knowledge that everything is made up, invented, usually out of tradition and authority. Although I will suggest that, in rock and roll, the dandy's aestheticism demystifies the cowboy's realism, I will also show that the cowboy's realism is the plain and ironic function of its dependence on prior texts. Here the burdensome knowledge of precedent with which we are familiar in Romantic tradition—my reading of Emerson will describe it—joins with the same grave and familiar wisdom in blues tradition, even, as we shall see throughout, at the level of technique. A rebuttal of Romanticism, black urbanity also rejoins with Romanticism when Romanticism itself is read—as we will read it—as an ironic enterprise, too. Urban dandyism or aestheticism, after all, does what black urbanity does—it substitutes the city for the country. It demystifies the myth of the American West and with it the agrarian myth of America at large, including its Southern American variant.

The African-American reversal of the Romantic paradigm makes clear what is at work within the Romantic paradigm all along: the undoing of its own presumptions to truth, the denaturing of all assumption, a reminder for all presumably natural communities to be cautious about how easy it is to seek in nature a cause and justification for anything. So dominant is this pattern in Romantic and blues traditions alike that it organizes any number of defining sites in their respective histories. What better model with which to assess the structure of Romantic freedom—Romanticism's most vaunted trope—than the structure of the belated and ironic freedom of African Americans?

IT IS, OF COURSE, difficult to narrate a dialectical argument in a linear fashion. This study is therefore organized as a series of juxtaposed historical meditations on the structure of crossing over that blues and Romantic traditions share. It is designed, much as a work of fiction is, to prompt a desire for the next piece of the story to emerge. My chronological narrative of each tradition is subtended by the discovery behind or beneath it of a similar rhetorical or semiotic paradigm—a loop or a crossing—as I trace the history of blues tradition after World War II and the history of Romanticism from Shelley to Emerson, Pater, and literary modernism. The paradigm of the country and the city organizes blues tradition much as the paradigm of the cowboy and the dandy organizes Romantic tradition. I begin my history in chapter 1 with a remarkably symbolic recording session in Clovis, New Mexico in 1958, deriving from the collaboration of Buddy Holly and Curtis Ousley not only the way that rock and roll crosses cowboy and dandy, country and city, country and blues, but also the way in which country and city structure the world of African-American music and culture at large, producing a discourse about the making and unmaking of boundaries very like Romanticism's own. By means of the country and the city, blues tradition—and behind it, as its engine, black urbanity—emerges as an ironic mode of imaginative compensation strikingly similar to that of Romanticism.

High Romanticism itself has a dual legacy in England and America respectively, a dual legacy that gives this study its title, a pop or mythological progeny that crystallized conceptually around those central Romantic figures, Emerson and Pater respectively, who give each mythology its fullest expression: in America, through Emerson, the mythology of the American West; in England, behind and through Pater (including a French entr'acte), the mythology of aestheticism. I will show how cowboy and dandy, Emerson and Pater are versions of one other and how their presumably different accents belie a profound similarity that joins them at the level of theme and structure alike. What they share—and what they share with blues tradition—is a common focus on boundaries and the active dynamic of crossing over. In chapter 2, I prosecute the rhetoric of Romanticism in detail, closely cross-examining Shelley's "Mont Blanc," Buffalo Bill's autobiography, and Emerson's essays before surveying the history of the cowboy and the history of Western mythology at large in the chapter's second half.

Urban or electric blues is the focus of chapter 3, which includes a reading of Muddy Waters and an assessment of Chuck Berry within an electric blues context. I turn to the dandy's own history in chapter 4, which also contains a reading of Pater and, at chapter's close, a consideration of the dandy detective, Sherlock Holmes. I then turn to three great rhythm and blues singers in chapter 5—Jackie Wilson, Smokey Robinson, and Al Green—before moving on to Willa Cather's novels in chapter 6. In chapter 7, I examine Miles Davis and the continuity between jazz and rock and roll before returning, in chapter 8, to the question of literary modernism, conducting there an examination of Virginia Woolf's fiction to show, as I do with Cather's, how continuous High Modernism on both sides of the Atlantic is with the Romanticism that enables it. Why Cather and Woolf? Because, as with Miles Davis's influence and achievement, their futures have made them canonical. Genuine late Romantics both, Cather and Woolf are the supreme examples in the modern novel of the Romantic line that moves from Shelley to Emerson and Pater. Much as the cowboy's outwardness and the dandy's inwardness are really inverse versions one of the other, so Woolf's inwardness and Cather's outlandishness, if I may put it that way, are interdependent or crossing structures, too, each focusing as a rule on boundaries, differences, enabling discrepancies. In chapter 9, I turn, finally, to a series of bands and artists in later rock and roll history, beginning with the British Invasion, including the Beatles, in 1964–66, and concluding with Jimi Hendrix, Bob Dylan, Led Zeppelin, and the Ramones.

Rather than present Sixties rock and roll and beyond as a grand summation or dialectical resolution of Romantic and blues traditions, however, I have chosen instead to present it as the elaboration of blues tradition that it is. While it is my contention throughout that rock and roll is a cross-cultural sensibility, I will not attempt, as others have done, to assess its history or its status as a presumable style of life (see, for example, Hebdige 1979). My focus is principally a focus on texts. Like the history of the black cowboy, for example, or the history of the dandy as a sociological phenomenon, the actual history of rock and roll subculture is outside the domain of this study, since my concerns address mythology and aesthetics within a number of historical traditions rather than empirical history or history as such. Music history is far more semiotically porous than the history of literature, especially the history of postclassical music such as jazz, rhythm and blues, and rock and roll. Its determinations, like those of film history, are more manifold. Because of this overdetermination, this porousness of field, rock and roll historiography and criticism can, like the music itself, take any number of possible routes, even that of a formalist's historiography garnished with meaningful incident. There are therefore inevitable as well as calculated omissions in the pages that follow. I discuss Jackie Wilson, Ray Charles, and Chuck Berry at some length, but I only allude to Phil Spector and Elvis; I focus on the history of electric guitar from Charlie Christian through punk, but I leave off the history of saxophone with some remarks about John Coltrane. I allude to African pre-texts, but I do not elaborate them, staying instead within an American geography. I presume the relative hegemony of the country and the city as an organizing motif in African-American culture, even though black settlements in the North have pasts of their own. I conclude my histories of both Romantic and blues traditions well before the present moment, curtailing my handling of Romantic culture with Cather and Woolf rather than proceeding on to an examination of postwar British or American fiction, and halting my study of rock and roll in the late 1970s with the Ramones, simply suggesting the reverberations of our paradigm in hip hop, for example, or its presence in bands like Nirvana.

How does this perspective modify our view of the relation between high culture and pop? This is not a task I have set for myself. The notion of a popular culture presumably distinct from a high culture is, of course, an invention of cultural establishments and an object of study in its own right. Like the study of rock and roll subculture or even the study of rock and roll performance in the narrow sense, its pursuit is beyond the aims of the present volume, too, although I should note what its contours may be in the case of the specific histories with which we are concerned. The late Romantic modernism of Woolf, say, or Cather freely and frankly continues the genuine Romantic tradition of Shelley and Wordsworth, Emerson and Pater, particularly a sense of life that well represents how implicated in culture we are, especially in our desire to move beyond it. It also well illustrates a relation between high and pop cultures that recalls Wordsworth's originary Romantic revolution of turning to the vernacular to understand how our sense of experience is ironically fashioned by those very structures of culture that supposedly constrain or inhibit it. The anti-Romantic modernism of Pound and Eliot, by contrast, shuts down precisely this relation between imagi-

nation and the social world that the late Romantic modernism of
Woolf and Cather does not (see Meisel 1987). It is also what pro-
hibits a relation between cowboy and dandy until the advent of rock
and roll in Romantic culture. Hence Dylan's description of Pound
and Eliot on "Desolation Row": "Fighting in the captain's tower /
While calypso singers laugh at them / And fishermen hold flowers"
(1965b). Pound and Eliot's parochial modernism seeks a justification
for its stance through the assertion of absolute laws of value. Anglo-
American English departments turn it into a durable religion of form
after World War II; the Beats turn it into a stupefying religion of nature. Even Lionel Trilling and the New Critics share a common root
in Matthew Arnold rather than in Paterian aestheticism. The birth
of rock and roll in postwar blues tradition is framed historically by
the rise of the New Criticism and the rise of Beat aesthetics, those
unlikely bedfellows that between them drive genuine Romantic culture to seek another route, another ground for its energies apart
from dominant culture alone. This route is well described by Pater's
term *Andersstreben,* or other-striving (1877, 54), the tendency of impulses garnered in the tradition of one medium—in this case literature—to follow themselves out or to cross over into another—in this
case music. It is also the route that Pound and Eliot forbid. With the
frontier closed and parochial modernism checking the Romantic
impulse within approved channels, the alternative of jazz in the
1920s—even Eliot recognizes it in poetic practice—and rock and roll
in the 1950s is altogether necessary for Romantic spiritual survival.
Why did Pound fail to relish his Idaho birth?

Here, of course, the vexing question of the relation of rock lyrics
to the English poetic tradition finally catches up with us—I had
sought to avoid it. How to study the verbal superstructure of a self-
consciously poetic rock and roll, however, constitutes, like the question of a popular culture, a specific area of inquiry in its own right,
and one that I have addressed only briefly, in my discussion of Bob
Dylan in chapter 9. Rock poets like Dylan or Kurt Cobain are inter-
esting as poets often to the extent that they are ineffective as poets
in the conventional sense of the word. It is their *Andersstreben*—
their Romanticism in a combination of media—that defines their
achievement, particularly the crossing of singing and language that
provides the setting for the exercises in vocal stress and obliquity of
accent that grant them an originality not to be found in their use of

lyric form alone. A resistance to *Andersstreben* may by the same token explain why American literary postmodernism has never fully explored the jazz and rock vein opened in it by Thomas Pynchon and Ishmael Reed, leaving the institution of the American novel to founder in a tepid psychological realism that still fails to take seriously the black advantage available to American writing. The equivocations of British postmodernism or Anglophone postcolonialism are, of course, even less promising; aestheticism has a more legitimate progeny in the Beatles than in Jeanette Winterson or Michael Ondaatje.

This is, however, a speculative history, not a totalizing one, a study of texts, not a study of manners or mores. What methodological problems may arise over the course of our discussion will be examined in a coda on canonicity and mythology, including my presumption that mythologies are the reduced rather than vulgarized social beliefs and practices that are customarily derived from canonical works of art (see Foucault 1969), especially if one includes, as Harold Bloom does (1994), the Bible and the sciences among them. Nor, of course, is this study strictly a historical one either. Ironically, our historical paradigm—cowboy and dandy, country and city—is itself a synchronic model based on the structure of crossing over that both Romantic and blues traditions share. Indeed, the very notion of historical paradigm is an oxymoron. Here, at the borders of our argument, the historical depends upon the frame, the temporal upon the static. This recurrent structure is, of course, a familiar one: it is a loop or a crossing over. This study as a whole is a loop or a crossing, folding back over or upon itself in any series of ways. The similarities that cowboy and dandy, country and city may have are themselves the belated, retroactive effect of the influence of African-American mythology upon Romantic imagination, and of the belated, retroactive effect of the machinery of cowboy and dandy, and of Romanticism at large, upon the design of black imagination. What follows is a narrative sequence whose overlays produce the familiar image of rock and roll in its numerous complexities.

1

the COUNTRY and the CITY

King Curtis and the Structure of Black Urbanity

L et us turn to another site in the West, some seventy years after Wilde's visit to Colorado. The time is September 1958; the place, a recording studio in Clovis, New Mexico. There is a cowboy and there is a dandy. One is Buddy Holly, singing a tune called "Reminiscing"; the other is "King" Curtis Ousley, tenor saxophonist from New York and inventor of yakety sax, joining Buddy for the recording session. A tight, foxy oompah tune written by Curtis (it was released under Holly's name only posthumously, in August of 1962), "Reminiscing" requires an almost electric crispness from the horn, and Curtis discovers a yakety way to deliver it with a remarkable and surprising freshness, very different from the honk-heavy repetitions of early rock and roll sax, and a style formalized by Curtis's lead horn on the Coasters' hit single "Yakety Yak" earlier in the same year. To say that Curtis dresses up Buddy's sound (as he did the sound of so many artists, including that of Aretha Franklin, the Shirelles, and Wilson Pickett) is an apt and historically exact metaphor to use to describe both the tune and the larger genesis of Curtis's horn.

What were King Curtis and Buddy Holly doing together in Clovis in 1958? Norman Petty's studio in Clovis was a fairly booming recording center in its own right (Gillett 1970, 96 ff.), although it is Holly who had invited Curtis to join him in New Mexico after they had worked together on a tour with the disc jockey Alan Freed in 1957 (see Norman 1996, 220; see also Goldrosen and Beecher 1986, 108). The act of imagination involved in bringing rock and roll together so completely is astonishing. Rock and roll history already shows its full hand of determinations, and out West to boot. Here two masters meet: the hiccuppy cowboy at one extreme, and, at the other, the dandy, the suave Manhattanite. What is most striking about King Curtis's horn on "Reminiscing" is in fact its urbanity. By contrast, Buddy's voice is, albeit in high manner, the voice of a hick, a yokel, a wailing swain. Country and western, rhythm and blues, cowboy and dandy, voice and horn all conjoin here. Lubbock, Texas, Buddy's birthplace, is across the border from Clovis and is high plains cowboy country. Buddy was himself a product of Texas swing, rockabilly, and bluegrass. He had learned banjo and man-dolin as a youngster, as well as Hank Williams's style of yodeling, the precursor sound to his own vocal signature. Of course, like Southern Baptist religion (see Bloom 1992), country music is incon-ceivable without a central African-American influence, however re-pressed or obscured (see Malone 1985). Country reconstitutes its principal European sources—spirituals, English and Irish ballad and jig, and Central European polka—by strongly misreading them through an otherwise silent African-American presence (the gospel phrasing is where it is overt; see Jones 1963, 46–47), a presence that becomes obvious only after Texas swing starts using saxophones in the 1930s. No wonder the Grand Ole Opry radio broadcasts were as popular among black audiences as among white (see Guralnick 1979). Common labor of the oppressed, country music and rhythm and blues have always enjoyed, as the saying goes, the same gospel and Delta roots; Waylon Jennings was even a member of Buddy's band.

It is, of course, a staple of rock criticism to observe that rock and roll is the crossing of country and blues traditions (see, for example, Marcus 1975, 162 ff.), although now the larger and stricter historical logic behind the proposition—and behind rock and roll's relation to Romanticism—also comes into focus. Rock and roll is the crossing of cowboy and dandy. If you grew up on Westerns and Sherlock Holmes, your destiny was rock and roll. And if the outwardness and aggression of the cowboy had a historical counterpart, it was, not surprisingly in retrospect, the inwardness and languor of the dandy. Dandy foppishness relieves and controls what strength there is in cowboy panache. Each leavens the other. You can see both at play in the semiotics as well as in the music of rock and roll. Little Richard,

Jimi Hendrix, Prince—all balance in a single style the cowboy's strength, the dandy's charm; the cowboy's rage, the dandy's melancholia. Even the British opposition between fashionable mods and tough rockers in the mid-Sixties recapitulates it. Chuck Berry shows how central and enabling the crossing is by using "country guitar lines adapted," in Robert Christgau's words, "to blues-style picking" (1972, 143). Like Elvis before him, Dylan, too, combines country with urban—a double lineage of Woody Guthrie and white folk on the one hand and Muddy Waters and the blues on the other—in an equally decisive instance of the crossing, especially after he decided to work with an electric band at the Newport Folk Festival in 1965. With their cowboy boots and dandy scarves, how like Wilde in Colorado Dylan and Elvis both are! Simply put, the blend of cowboy and dandy is suddenly unavoidable in rock and roll. Group monikers like Guns 'N Roses or the Sex Pistols only formalize what is already at play in the prehistory of a discourse so overdetermined as to produce both the Beatle boot and an extended meditation on the leopard-skin pillbox hat (see Dylan 1966).

But wait. Rock and roll as a crossing or combination of cowboy and dandy may be a sweet enough conjecture from the point of view of dominant or Romantic culture. But is it true from the point of view of African-American culture, especially if country and blues alike are forms of African-American music? By the same token, if country and blues are both part of blues tradition, then rock and roll as a crossing of cowboy and dandy is an altogether fair way to describe the manner in which it crosses two strands within blues tradition itself, country on the one hand and blues proper on the other. Then again, why is King Curtis in the role of dandy at Clovis next to Buddy the cowboy? Is some imperial misadventure afoot in such a formulation? Are cowboy and dandy even reasonable terms with which to describe African-American culture and its products? Here a whole new history emerges side by side with that of a dominant Romanticism and its vocabulary, and with it a whole new paradigm with which to organize rock and roll, its history, and its structure. The new paradigm, of course, is different from the Romantic one—I shall examine Romanticism in detail beginning in the next chapter—but it is also very similar to it. Like the Romantic paradigm, it is preoccupied with boundaries and with the way in which they get fashioned. Unlike the Romantic paradigm, however, its terms are drawn from a different kind of historical perspective. Let us follow King Curtis's route through the history of jazz to see just what it is before attending to the Romantic paradigm that is its analog or counterpart.

Curtis is responding to a crisis in jazz history that splits swing into two major strains after World War II. From its beginnings through swing, jazz was institutionally one thing, a form of public entertainment in which virtuosity was prized. After World War II, the legacy of swing divided this history into two new branches: bop or modern jazz, emphasizing the combo rather than the orchestra or big band; and rhythm and blues, which spirited away the big band sound and turned it, through many permutations, into rock and roll. Bop, of course, transformed jazz into a self-conscious art project that retained, God knows, its hard, swinging power, even though it encouraged—indeed, lionized—the emergence of the visionary soloist, allowing him "to fly," as Ira Gitler describes it, "with eighth-note constructions and extend [his] lines to include bursts of sixteenth and thirty-second notes" (1985, 5). The structure of bop chord changes added Euro-harmonics and modes to blues logic (see Russell 1960), and Charlie Parker's influence as a soloist and a harmonic thinker became, except for Louis Armstrong's, unparalleled in the history of jazz. Like Dizzy Gillespie's beret, Parker's jesting use of an English accent on the bandstand or on outtakes in the studio underscores the irony with which European tropes and stances were appropriated by the boppers, even though such poses were also the logical extension of Armstrong's morning coat and spats, or Cab Calloway's tails and white tie. By the same token, of course, Parker's Western side is so decisive a factor in the elements out of which he is made that this native of Kansas who had woodshedded in the Ozarks (not for nothing was his nickname Yardbird) had turned down Duke Ellington's offer to join his orchestra to work instead with the rawer Kansas City bandleader Jay McShann. Indeed, bebop itself is, at least in a Romantic vocabulary, a colossal crossing of cowboy and dandy, even though its imaginative power inspired as much anxiety as it did influence.

Rhythm and blues and its rock and roll progeny, by contrast, restored jazz to the level of pop entertainment from which it eventually fell thanks to jazz modernism. Rhythm and blues is a term for which many folks have taken credit, but it designates something clear and simple: a jump sound that people danced to beginning in the 1940s that often featured rocking saxophone leads free from the calculus of bop. The initial model for this jump sound is Louis Jordan, bandleader, altoist, and singer, who is, retrospectively, the great alternative to Parker, and who is the Great Divide between swing and an emergent rhythm and blues or rock and roll that is the second of swing's two children. "For the masses of blacks," writes Nelson George, "after bebop's emergence, jazz was respected, but in times of leisure and relaxation they turned to Louis Jordan" (1988, 25). George cites Jordan's growing slew of hit records from 1943 to 1947 to document the shift (1988, 5; for a similar account by three producers, see Hammond 1977; Wexler 1993; and Gordy 1994; see also Shaw 1978, 61.ff.). By the early 1950s, however, Jordan's sales on Decca begin to decline, and Earl Bostic's on King begin to rise as he eventually records more hits than Jordan in the same r & b mode, inheriting and expanding Jordan's audience and codifying the alto style associated with Jordan's band.

Although to compare Parker to Jordan and Bostic is to compare a mortal god with a pair of sergeant-majors, it is still fair to say that Jordan and Bostic are the line in the sand between bop and rock and roll itself. While Jordan forms the Tympany Five in 1938, late in the swing era (the bop jams at Minton's in Harlem begin in the early 1940s), the model of the small group playing rocking ensemble music rather than featuring the clash of soloing Titans establishes for the generation after swing an alterative to the bop combo and an alternative to the bop use of the solo horn. A variety of alto players handled the soloing in Jordan's orchestra, among them Jordan himself, and it is Bostic who goes on to stabilize under a single signature the solo sax sound that Jordan and his band introduce. From this point of view, rock and roll is, belatedly, really a reaction to bebop, a swerve from its anxieties (Jones locates another, less truculent reaction in the hard bop of Horace Silver and Art Blakey in the second half of the 1950s, following Parker's death in 1955 [1963, 216–17]). While rhythm and blues may have misread bebop by overestimating its intellectualism (some rockers still share the misapprehension), it nonetheless provided a way to steer clear of Parker's influence, either as a buffer against it (as in the funkier, Southern tradition of the chicken-shack combo featuring tenor and B-3 organ), or as a knowing choice, as the young John Coltrane's appearance with

Eddie "Cleanhead" Vinson at the Apollo in 1947 may suggest. Indeed, after apprentice work as Dizzy's alto sideman, Coltrane thickens the plot of his own reaction to Parker by joining the funk organist Jimmy Smith for two weeks in 1955 and then the organist Shirley Scott for two months, completing his tour with Scott only one month before joining Miles Davis as a tenorman later in the same year. He even records some standards with Bostic himself at a session in Cincinnati in April of 1952.

What is the technology of the Jordan sound that Bostic formalizes? Like Parker, Jordan and Bostic play alto with no vibrato, the sign of a common starting point as revisions of the same precursor, swing tenorman Lester Young (on Parker and vibrato, see Crouch 1983, 258), and of their different swerves from him. With Parker, the swerve is rhetorical and percussive alike; with Jordan and Bostic, however, the swerve is almost altogether percussive and the rhetoric a sparse version of the swing vocabulary they share with Parker. Like a blues shouter rather than a jazz singer, the tone and accent of Jordan's or Bostic's horn are notable more for their rhythmic timing than for their lyrical elaboration, reinventing phrasing in as epochal a reassignment as bop but with a very different kind of influence behind—and before—it. Jordan's vocal strategy, too, is knowingly bound, presaging James Brown and Sly Stone in the refusal of an easy liquidity. If Parker drives saxophone forward, beyond Lester Young, then Jordan and Bostic take it back within the Lester Young tradition but curtail and sharpen it, not unlike those honkdown saxophonists who predated or resisted the discipleship to Parker and who prefigure Curtis himself, Illinois Jacquet in particular. Even more than Jordan, Bostic is a genuine crossover figure who spans the hyperbolic vibrato of swing saxophone and the shocking brashness of the rock and roll instrument that emerges out of it, sometimes actually narrating the movement from one mode to the other over the course of a single tune, as he does on "What, No Pearls?," an original composition in which vibrato is isolated and converted into a yelping growl.

King Curtis perfects the Jordan-Bostic line—he doubtless knew Bostic in New York once he had settled there as a young session aspirant in the early 1950s—and shows how rock and roll can take the logic that invented jazz itself another step further. Long before his death in 1971, when he was fatally stabbed outside his home in Manhattan, Curtis had already transformed saxophone into a true rock and roll instrument because he had helped to solve the crisis of bop influence in jazz. As a youngster, he had toured with Lionel Hampton's orchestra, a gig thick with influences (Jacquet had played with Hampton, as had Bostic), and an atmosphere in which he came to recall jazz's own earlier state. Curtis puts this mode of recollection to work at the very center of his own sound. The result is not only still durable; it remains the paradigm for rock and roll saxophone even today, as the example of David Sanborn and other saxophonists more and more popular since the late 1970s makes plain (on Curtis's customary neglect, see Wexler 1993, 249).

The secret of Curtis's sound derives, ironically, from its use of country, and country and western, materials. Its urbanity is a paradoxical effect of its exploitation of rural styles, its suave city sound begotten, as it turns out, in Texas. King Curtis was originally from Fort Worth, and his yakety horn is an audacious transformation of what is customarily called Texas tenor, a broad, open sound like Jacquet's, a sound more stomping than the beboppers' despite their own profound bluesiness, and the jazz counterpart to the big, open stance of the cowboy himself. The dandy from New York has a country background and his horn a Texas pedigree. Buddy Holly and King Curtis are both from Texas, and the country influences central to Holly are central, too, in King Curtis's different use of them. Searching for an escape from bop, Curtis makes as radical a swerve from Parker as Coltrane does, although even the yakety style is itself a version of one of Parker's mannerisms that Sonny Rollins once called "pecking" (Davis 1989, 79). The direction is the style of the banjo, fiddle, and picking guitar—bluegrass styles adapted to horn usage. Fiddle and banjo had been widely used by African-American musicians before the Civil War, while in jazz bands in the twentieth century, banjo had been superseded by guitar by the late 1920s (Barlow 1989, 29–30). Fiddle and banjo alike were part of early Dixieland instrumentation, but both instruments were left largely behind to enjoy their presumably separate destiny in country music.

Curtis's stroke of insight is astonishing, and valued far less than it should be. If Parker becomes a dandy—learned, urban—to lift swing into a world of advanced harmonics that he can use jazz logic to transform, then Curtis becomes a cowboy—a hick, a stomping Texan all over again—to counter Parker's own urbanity and the overwhelming power of its influence upon jazz phrasing and changes. The country mode also allows Curtis to push the horn beyond Jordan's and Bostic's example, too, into a simpler, sharper, and more pointed percussive relation to a rocking rhythm section. It thereby opens up a new lyrical space for an otherwise merely rhythmic or percussive horn (there is also a touch of classical oboe tone that eases the percussive and the country alike). While on the one hand Curtis's horn is jagged, on the other it is so sweet, so vocal, and sometimes so lyrical—"Soul Serenade" (1964) is the best example— that its project may seem self-divided. This self-division, however, is a rock and roll strategy born of jazz necessity. Unlike Junior Walker, his nearest contemporary, Curtis doesn't just sweeten up Texas tenor; he also gives it a shear edge beyond Walker's dismissive growls. He does so by crossing the size of Texas tenor tone with the bite and timbre of Jordan's or Bostic's alto. In the process of resolving the influence of Texas tenor, he also resolves the influence of rhythm and blues alto, using one to deflect the other. Both nonbop descendants of swing saxophone, Curtis breeds them to move beyond bop and rhythm and blues alike, and as a means of attuning his own horn to the brassier country earliness he has in mind.

The stakes here are high, and they extend beyond jazz history proper. The (re)turn to country materials is not just an example of Curtis's swerve from bop. It is also an example of an imaginative strategy in black culture that blues tradition registers with particular clarity and that jazz and rock and roll each register in specific ways. Like Romantic imagination, it is, of course, a mode of crossing, although it is a crossing not of cowboy and dandy, East and West, but of city and country, North and South. Unlike the structure of Romantic imagination, it derives from a structure at work in the history of African-American culture, the difference between country and city engendered by the great migrations from South to North that move into high gear during World War I, when the need for industrial labor in a North deprived of its steady flow of European immigrants combines with the mechanization of cotton picking in the South and the deterioration of race relations there to attract Southern blacks to urban centers in ever increasing numbers. In 1900, 90 percent of all African Americans lived in the South (Davis 1991, 7); in 1940, the figure was 77 percent, and, by 1970, it was only half (Lemann 1991, 6; see also Douglas 1995, 312 ff.). And while the large migrations after World War II from the Southwest to the cities of California may not obey the literal geography of South and North, they also recapitulate the paradigm, since the mythos attending them is likewise informed not only by the opposition between bondage and freedom but by the urban disappointments that the West, too, can provide black Americans.

The migrations to the cities has the double and unsettling effect of disillusion in the promise of the North and a changed, newly self-conscious relation to the rural South, a relation possible only through the memory and imagination that estrangement from it ironically provides. Like black settlements in the West after the Civil War (see Katz 1971), the migrations North evacuate a typology even as they fulfill it. Moving North means nothing at all, except the clarification of a grim perspective. The structure of the geography, however, presents opportunities that the geography itself does not. It prompts a fresh cultural stance based on the new tie of association between North and South, a stance based on the structure of the relation or ambivalence between the two rather than on its resolution, and one that better estimates history than the typological stance of suffering and deliverance that experience has shown to be empty. The solution to the anxieties that accompany it is the imagination or invention of a new kind of urbanity, often by importing country styles to city modes, a way of suspending rather than reconciling the split or opposition between them. Dialectical or crossing, black urbanity is a Southern mode of Northerliness, a Northern mode of Southerliness, a kind of trick played at the crossroads that fends off the tension produced by being in an otherwise groundless situation. Banjo and fiddle styles are transferred to the urbanity of the saxophone, while saxophone welcomes its country cousins the banjo and the fiddle.

The invention and durability of a black urbanity based upon country styles is an achievement central to black imagination and to American imagination at large. The emergence of jazz in the 1920s is its first signature, and King Curtis's achievement in the 1950s is representative of black urbanity in a specifically rock and roll mode. To use the signifying title of a LaVern Baker tune upon which King Curtis also appeared, black urbanity produces a style of identity that exchanges Jim Crow for "Jim Dandy" (1956) and that is part of a tradition that produced band names like Zack White's Chocolate Beau

Brummells in the mid-1920s, or the Chocolate Dandies in the late 1920s, a band more often known as McKinney's Cotton Pickers. The cowboy and the dandy play their dialectical game in black culture, too, although they do so under the name of country and city. Curtis's use of country, for example, and his allegiance to the pop mode of rhythm and blues make him, like Jordan or Bostic before him, the cowboy next to Parker's dandy, the man of the people rather than the urban artist. But, of course, Parker himself is the American roughneck cowboy—the Kansas City stomper—next to the urban Euro-harmonics that are, like Henry James's or Willa Cather's English and French influences, his own dandy side as an American artist. Next to Buddy Holly, however, Curtis is not a cowboy, but is himself a dandy. Then again, Buddy, too, has crossed over, and more than once: he overcomes the influence of Hank Williams by hearing the blues, and he overcomes the influence of the blues by hearing Dean Martin (see Tosches 1992). Clovis presents us with a paradigm for rock and roll in 1958 that actually allows Curtis and Buddy each to play both roles, cowboy and dandy, at once, to control both perspectives by exploiting the structure of black urbanity that engenders rock and roll as a form, and whose earlier manifestation as jazz now takes a heightened turn. If Armstrong in the 1920s brings the country to the city, then postwar blues and rhythm and blues bring the city back to the country—the North, as it were, back to the South—in an even more self-conscious exercise of urban imagination upon country materials. By virtue of the comparisons that time itself provides, Armstrong's own journey from the country to the city is now more than ever the start of an endless dialectic between the two poles, not simply a passage from the one to the other.

As an ideological operation, of course, black urbanity also redacts the customary racial positioning of black in relation to white (see, for example, Fanon 1952) by casting white as brutish and black as civilized. At Clovis, with Curtis as dandy and Buddy as cowboy, black culture is no longer a preserve of savage energy managed, as in the Beatnik version, by a colonialist bohemia (see, for example, Mailer 1957; Kerouac 1958, 1959). No goad for drawing out raw, spontaneous energy in otherwise docile white folks, here black culture is instead the very sign of the city, of culture, while white culture is the sign of nature and lack of civilized control. By the same token, however, Clovis is parabolic because it doesn't simply reverse the customary roles; it also rearticulates the way in which structure itself may be said to function. Let us glance at how country and city structure black American culture—and how they can raise questions about cultural signification in the process—before turning to the nature of black urbanity as a compensatory mode of imagination and as a model for the emergence of rock and roll.

The course of blues tradition registers the history of the migrations with extraordinary clarity and even shows how major population shifts parallel key movements in the history of music. The period between 1900 and 1930 that changed the structure of the American census also changed the texture of American culture (Katznelson 1973, 310); it frames the new hegemony of blues music in an urban mode—jazz—that crystallizes with the conversion of country blues into classic blues. When the New Orleans native Louis Armstrong joined the Fletcher Henderson orchestra in 1924, "he taught New York," in Gary Giddins's words, "to swing" (1988, 81). The period between the two world wars saw the birth of a black metropolis in Chicago (see Drake and Cayton 1945) and the emergence of swing in Kansas City (for an account, see Russell 1971). Between 1940 and 1970, the population profile changed drastically again, and once again the "paradigm shift," as Nicholas Lemann calls the uneasiness of country and city (1991, 40), was reflected on the stages of Chicago's own clubs: "Musically," writes Lemann, "the South Side of Chicago was ruled by the dapper, mustachioed, pomaded Muddy Waters, the West Side by the raw, overwhelming, enormous Howlin' Wolf" (83), both sons of the Delta and between them structuring Chicago cultural life as a play between electric blues versions of dandy and cowboy.

The stance of a rugged, cowboy dandyism, the new urbanity leads, of course, to the creation of African-American show business (Morgan and Barlow 1992) and rewrites a prehistory in minstrelsy that jazz manner and costume have already evoked (see also Stearns and Stearns 1968). Black urbanity reappropriates and reimagines the caricatured rivalry between "plantation" and "dandy" blacks as depicted in white minstrel shows as early as the 1820s (Southern 1971, 89) and opens an entire field of mythographic construction to the needs of reinvention (for Stephen Foster's response beginning in the 1840s, see Emerson 1995). Indeed, later nineteenth-century black minstrelsy and black independent theater (see Johnson 1930) feature a tradition of ironic performance whose mimicries, parodies, and mockeries of Romantic culture also raise central questions about the very status of familiar tropes within our historical materials themselves, especially when we ask whether such Romantic mythologies as cowboy and dandy apply to a historiography of the oppressed, and what it means to say that country and city are versions of cowboy and dandy when Howlin' Wolf and Muddy Waters are playing (see, for example, Bhabha 1994). One is reminded of Henry Louis Gates, Jr.'s, notion that black culture disrupts the very logic of normative signification by using it in a new way (1988, 47 ff.).

To raise the question of whether it is fair to assign to African-American culture a position of revising Romantic culture is, of course, also to raise the opposite question: whether it is fair to read African-American culture through the tropes of Romanticism. These are the signature preoccupations of W. E. B. Du Bois, and they structure both the questions he asks and the ways in which he asks them. Du Bois's paradigmatic discovery of the country in *The Souls of Black Folk* (1903) is an ironic function of his urbanity as both a Northerner and an intellectual. Like the Latin phrases used to praise Africa in his speeches, the Romantic invocations of the rural folk here serve to heighten the contrasts out of which the book's extraordinary textures are made, chief among them a system of double epigraphs for each chapter that juxtaposes musical notations from black spirituals and texts from Romantic or late-Romantic literature. Even Du Bois's invention of a pan-African identity over the later course of his career is the durable sign of his Euromodernism, based as it is on both his training in German philosophy and his estrangement from it.

But like the paradox of country and city, Du Bois's paradoxes are structures of oppression that he converts into salutary new structures of imaginative power. The "double-consciousness" that is the notorious problem—"this sense of always looking at one's self through the eyes of others" (1903, 5)—becomes the ground for its own solution. "What was initially felt to be a curse," as Gilroy describes it, "gets repossessed" (1993, 111). There is, alas, no "true self-consciousness" in the first place, only "double-consciousness" from the start; no primary self, only a social self made up of reflection. Like Romanticism—we shall see this at length later on—it exposes the split subjectivity of master and slave alike (see Habermas 1985;

see also Žižek 1989). Mastery is subdued, to use the sound-recording metaphor, by remastering, and the ego itself is subdued into ecstasy. If the historical "humiliation" that has produced the situation is "studied," as a punning Du Bois puts it (174), then the yield is this new kind of learning.

Du Bois's paradoxical preoccupations structure the history of African-American studies (see Baker 1984) and the ideological split between Eurocentrism and Afrocentrism that presumably divides it despite the obvious complementarity of the two approaches. Indeed, Du Bois's early criticisms of Booker T. Washington include Washington's inability to see paradox as constitutive in historical process. Paradox, however, is also central, as it were, to Washington himself, whose autobiography is structured from its very beginning by a crossing that gives it its logic and its force as it moves toward a remarkable and uncanny conclusion. "Born near a cross-roads post-office" as a slave (1901, 1), Washington the elderly gentleman discovers an edition of Frederick Douglass's autobiography in the library of a steamship at book's close (288). Washington's achievement ironically narrates the return to a precursor. Nor is the return immediate; the earlier comes in the form of a text. The primary and the secondary are functions of one another. The latecomer is not burdened by the pioneer, nor the pioneer by the latecomer. The relation itself is the enabling invention, not a choice between one or the other of the alternatives it presents. Washington, too, is paradigmatic. The interdependence of past and present is the interdependence of country and city in another key, and it renders the proverbial debate about country and city, urban and folk in black culture and black studies a structural inevitability rather than a debate about real choices.

Or consider Langston Hughes's poem "Aesthete in Harlem" (1930). Hughes gives us a title that already has us wondering whether an impulse to read its signifiers as a juxtaposition is justified, and whether the ambiguity says as much about the reader as it does about the text. Does the poem go on, then, to banish the aesthetic, or does it reinvent it? Are "aesthete" and "Harlem" at odds, or are they put into relation in a new way? It is not, after all, until the poet comes to "this near street" (6)—in Harlem, a metonym, presumably—that he finds the "life" (7) that he cannot find in "places gentler speaking" (5). Country and city seem to reappear in the midst of the city itself as the difference between uptown and downtown. But this is an easy reading of the poem, and one that it does not sustain. A newer, rawer sense of life is already available to the poet here precisely because it "step[s]" on his "feet" (7). The play on words—"feet" are also poetic figures—prompts the recognition that the sanctification of the quotidian is an achievement in the very forms it appears to spurn. The poem cannot sustain either of its terms without the other. Whichever sense we give the poem requires that we exile—hence include, however negatively or silently—its rejoinder. The poem's structure is really the rotation of possibilities in an endless crossing back and forth. Like the opposition of cowboy and dandy, the opposition of country and city, funky and falutin', constantly turns inside out, each pole a function or a foil of the other.

This doubleness or interdependence of country and city is perhaps most familiar in the history of African-American fiction. The African-American novel as a rule brings to bear any series of Eurocentric techniques upon black *mythoi* and experience, and simultaneously takes the results straightforwardly and ironically. Much as King Curtis combines country and city, so Zora Neale Hurston, for example, reflects on country materials in *Their Eyes Were Watching God* (1937) with an anthropologist's zeal and the resources of American modernism. The power of Richard Wright's *Native Son* (1940) derives in no small measure from its ironic reimagination of black experience through the tradition of naturalism from Zola to Dreiser, a way of really driving the nature of Bigger's predicament home by showing it to be at bottom the function of an aesthetic inevitability with which the political is, outrageously enough, actually identical. Ralph Ellison's *Invisible Man* (1950) is not only an equivalent reimagination of black experience through the techniques of Kafkan modernism. It is also a reimagination of the way Wright himself reveals the identity of the aesthetic and the existential, the formal and the political. In all three cases, the difference between country and city, life and literature, reality and myth is simultaneously maintained and dismantled. This tendency abides, of course, in Alice Walker and Toni Morrison, although Ishmael Reed takes the strategy much further by breaking down exponential versions of these oppositions, whether between the rival discursive regimes of cowboy and dandy, Loop Garoo and Hoodoo Too, in *Yellow Back Radio Broke-Down* (1969), or between fixity and crossover as the rival interpretative modes of Aton and Jes Grew in *Mumbo Jumbo* (1972). Even James Baldwin's stark oppositions of country and city, cowboy and dandy, black and white in *Another Country* (1962) turn out to be vengefully reciprocal. The presumable purity of white is, of course, the function of comparison, too.

But whatever black urbanity's undecidable relation to Romanticism—a revision of it or an entirely separate growth—it redoubles Romanticism in structure and dynamic. Black urbanity is an empowering imaginative invention that controls both perspectives, the country and the city, at once and, like Romantic imagination, takes its power from a crossing or contamination of perspectives that lends each perspective its effect. Like Romanticism, it, too, is a mode of imaginative compensation that bestows a leverage in power upon the fortunate latecomer by providing an instrument of memorial mastery or control of the past from a combination of two otherwise powerless points of view. The structure of black urbanity is one of deferred action, to use Freud's term (1918, 17:45), a structure designed to reestimate the past from the point of view of later experience and, in the process, to gain a new and empowering perspective over historical materials. It is a mode of "re-memory" or "re-membering," as Toni Morrison's narrator calls it in *Beloved* (1987, passim), the production of "new pictures" (95) to "beat . . . back the past" (73), a way to "change the leaving" (223), making "coming . . . the reverse route of going" (263). Curtis's tune is not called "Reminiscing" for nothing. The mastery of memory reevaluates the South and the past by seeing, after the fact and from the point of view of the North and the future, what value there was in country experience as distinct from its overwhelming miseries and the endless shadows they cast. The result is an endorsement of neither North nor South, but the discovery of double or crossing perspective itself. "[T]here is the world of comparisons," writes Alice Walker, "between town and country," the "double vision" of the black artist (1970, 18, 19). When Albert Murray writes of the sweetness of the South—a "cozy and cuddly time Down South all over the world" (1971, 27)—it is as a place in the mind, not, finally, as a real territory. bell hooks even splits her narrator between two pronouns—"I" and "she"—in a memoir recalling her Southern girlhood (1996). Simultaneous country and city vision suspends the calamitous force of Southern historical experience while also preserving the cultural forms that emerged from it, especially blues tradition and an originary sense of community that grew imperiled in the moves North.

The South signifies what the historian Pierre Nora calls a *lieu de mémoire*, or site of memory, the term favored to describe the mechanism of black urbanity by Geneviève Fabre and Robert O'Meally in their collection *History and Memory in African-American Culture* (1994). Black urbanity structures the way in which a site of memory may, in Melvin Dixon's words, "contribute to the process of cultural recovery" (1994, 19) by "deconstructing," as the editors put it, "a subversive *lieu de mémoire* and now constructing another" to replace it (1994, 12). Black urbanity at one and the same time cancels and preserves history, taking advantage of the temporality that resituates the South from the belated point of view of the North. In an example of what Nora calls the "reciprocal overdetermination" of "memory and history" that creates *lieux de mémoire* (1994, 295), Hurston, for example, "define[s] . . . a rural folk," as Hazel Carby describes it, by "measur[ing] them and their cultural forms against an urban, mass culture." Indeed, "[t]he creation of a discourse of the 'folk' as a *rural* people in Hurston's work in the twenties and thirties displaces the migration of black people to cities" (1994, 31). Like a collective version of Freud's primal scene (1918, 17:39), the *lieu de mémoire* is a retroactively generated origin, an earlier place that comes into being as a function of the distance that estranges you from it. Hence its liberating as well as symptomological possibilities. "Tradition," writes Nora, "is memory that has become historically aware of itself" (1992, ix).

The opposition between country and city is also equivalent to the crucial opposition in black culture between sacred and secular, another opposition that black urbanity topples by crossing its poles. Of the terms and images available to describe the movement from South to North historically, the biblical ones are, of course, most frequently used, even though—or perhaps because—"the sacred world," as Lawrence Levine puts it, was "never again to occupy the central position of the antebellum years" (1977, 191). Citing Bercovitch (1978), Baker notes the extent to which biblical typology informs African-American as well as colonial experience (1984, 20–21), especially, so the remarkable implication goes, as a means of overcoming the putatively Greek mythos of the plantation tradition

(130). Typology and geography can, however, also lead to confusion and to a recognition of the extraordinary pliability of typological tradition. Country and city do not, alas, apply to the structure of East and West in American Romanticism. Here two interpretations of biblical protocol vie for priority as to whose version of secular correspondence is correct. In American Romanticism and its typological tradition, it is the West, the country, that is free, and the East, the city, that is bondage. In African-American culture, it is the South, the country, that is bondage, and the North, the city, that is free. Here Frederick Douglass's famous narrative of 1845 prefigures our entire paradigm, with innocence and knowledge taking the roles of country and city under the cloak of typology. The fall from the primacy of the Edenic rural South into the history embodied by the cities is the fall from a plenitude that never existed in the first place. Douglass's rhetoric contests the very myth of origins that it presumably (re)presents, "a symbolically inverted account," as Baker puts it, "of the Fall of Man" (1984, 42; see also Gates 1978). Douglass's "fall" into writing actually reverses the categorical structures of normative representation because it reorganizes the customary relationship between nature and culture—or country and city—by crossing or exchanging their qualities.

It is, of course, rock and roll's marriage of gospel and blues, especially gospel singing over blues rhythms, that best represents its urbane solution to the differences that country and city characteristically represent. Hence another crossing, and one that also accounts for what we think of as an originary rock and roll sound. Rock and roll is gospel, or religious, vocal phrasing over blues, or secular, rhythm sections, a fusion—and, simultaneously, an undoing—of the opposition between sacred and secular, country and city, nature and culture, a way of being in both places at the same time. Hence, too, the revisionary use of the big sound of the Hammond B-3 organ (together with tenor saxophone and drums) in chickenshack roadhouses in the religious South, a fine swerve from church organ and an emblem for the new climate that blends swing or jazz protocols with sacred ones.

Ray Charles is a more familiar and decisive figure than King Curtis himself, and his sound is the fullest measure of the success of crossing gospel voice and blues rhythms, a crossing structurally equivalent to the crossing of country and blues (Charles's country mode now looks more logical, too). "Ray broke down the division between pulpit and bandstand," writes George (1988, 70); Murray argues that such secularization goes at least as far back as Armstrong (1976, 30 ff). Like Curtis's retrograde synthesis of two presumably opposed modes or vocabularies, Charles's achievement is based squarely on the use of gospel or country phrasing over swing or city time. It is also an example of how he overcomes Nat Cole's enabling jazz influence by flight to another mode, much as Curtis overcomes Parker's by a similar strategy. Charles's vocal genius also stages the breakdown of another critical opposition that will become more and more central to us as rock and roll history progresses, the difference between voice and instrument. Like the difference between secular and sacred, gospel and blues, cowboy and dandy, this customary difference, too, gets crossed or undone by the fact that Charles's voice, like Armstrong's, is itself an instrument of surpassing technique. It also suggests the active strategy of rock and roll imagination to be the calculated confusion of any series of familiar oppositions, usually or particularly musical ones, and including, as we shall see, epistemological ones extraordinarily similar to those at work in Romanticism.

The logic of black urbanity is even plain in the invention of the backbeat, another example of how rock and roll takes black urbanity a step further than jazz. The new rock and roll or funk rhythms that emerge in the 1950s enact a dynamic of influence that joins not just city and country or North and South but also North America and Latin, specifically Caribbean, America. Connie Kay, jazz and session drummer, tells the story of a rock and roll recording date that required him, when the piano player didn't show, to add a second beat on the bass drum (Giddins 1995). The result: the (d)evolution of the swing beat into the funk beat. But how? The extra beat that was added to the swing beat by the bass drum was in fact the sound of conga. Afro-Cuban in origin, conga had often been used with bop swing rhythms by Dizzy Gillespie. Now, however, bop's use of conga is transformed by rock and roll. Rock and roll incorporates conga more drastically, more decisively into the rhythm by having the bass drum play the conga's quarter notes. This is the other side of the bass drum's mimicry of Sousa, the addition of the Afro-Cuban double beat to a swing bottom; it brings cultural compensation full circle and makes the backbeat a genuinely cosmopolitan achievement, far more than bop's colonization of conga under the sign of the swinging ride cymbal. Jazz and session drummer Panama Francis observes that the bass drum keeps time in swing but not in bop, where the ride cymbal predominates as a metric device (Deffaa 1989, 175 ff.). In rock and roll, however, the bass drum regains its central position, although now with a difference in accent, the likely result of incorporating the sound of the conga into the trap set and its transistorization of the marching band. The rhythm section on the Beatles' "Nowhere Man" (1966a) well exemplifies Francis's point: McCartney's bass both walks and accents the second beat of the 2/4 time (Ringo accents on the bass drum along with Paul only on the second beat, too), simultaneously preserving a swing bottom while also overthrowing it in favor of a backbeat stress.

Black urbanity's ironic strength is what makes rock and roll mechanisms so supple and what allows rock and roll to take blues tradition into a kind of overdrive. Whether country and city, sacred and secular, North and South, or voice and instrument, the very crossing of the opposition also undoes or unties it. In Charles's case, vocal technique actually exchanges the very terms of the opposition as it exercises them. This crossing dynamic is the key to black culture's simultaneous cancellation and preservation of dominant ideological modes and the mechanism that rock and roll takes particular advantage of as an imaginative strategy. Jones even remarks that the emergence of rhythm and blues is the later symbol of the same "urban tradition" that Armstrong originally represents (1963, 155 ff.). If jazz comes to the city from the country, then rock and roll comes back to the country from an experience of the city. It crosses back again. The words of "I Shall Be Released" apply to city and country, cowboy and dandy alike: "I see the light come shining / From the West down to the East" (1968). Rock and roll's very belatedness—its coming after jazz, especially after bop—is what gives it its earliness. If jazz brought the South to the North, now rock and roll brings the North back to the South, after the fact. To cross to the country from the city, from the West back to the East, is, in a manner of speaking, to dandify the cowboy, to acknowledge influence, to orchestrate an irony.

2

WILDE WEST

What Wilde and the Westerners shared, of course, was the license that Romanticism afforded and that cowboy and dandy each exploited in a different way. Between them was the Romantic bond that Wilde teased out, the bond with their dandy counterparts that Americans in general, and Westerners in particular, couldn't quite admit to themselves: that the great outdoors was really an elaborate form of interior decoration. The cultivation of both exterior space and internal reflection depends upon a single principle of imperial imagination. "A continuous redistribution of matter and motion," as a Paterian Wilde puts it in 1879 (9:183), three years before his American trip, is the visionary imperative that links science and art, the practical and the imaginative, the American and the European, the cowboy and the dandy. Like the artist, the American—so the implication goes as Wilde delivered this apothegm to an audience in Washington in June of 1882, just before heading West—"will take from his surroundings whatever is salutary for his own spirit" (1882b, 11:119).

Shelley's "Mont Blanc," written in 1816, is a text fundamental to both the American and the British reception of High Romanticism and a poem that well exemplifies Wilde's notion of Shelley— "the blue cavern of an echoing deep" (1881, 1:190). It also well exemplifies the strategic regularities of Romantic imagination at large. What are they, and how do they work? After trying to convince both himself and his reader that Mont Blanc is, to adapt Lionel Trilling's phrase about the self, a realm beyond culture, Shelley closes the poem with a startling reversal as he asks the mountain a question:

> And what were thou, and earth, and stars, and sea,
> If to the human mind's imaginings
> Silence and solitude were vacancy? (142–44)

Silence and solitude are not, however, "vacancy," thanks to the power of imagination. Then again, "vacancy," too, is a reading of nature, a prop upon which imagination can build with even greater arrogance. As Wilde makes clear later on, the imagination stirs nature into life, not the other way around. Shelley, however, comes to this precipice of thought only negatively, provocatively demystifying at the end of the poem what he has spent most of the poem trying to achieve—a vision of this alpine majesty as pure and unsullied.

Although Shelley's "trance sublime" (35), as he puts it earlier, is an opportunity "[t]o muse on my own separate fantasy" (36), this solipsism is merely heuristic, a way to get things going. In an anticipation of Pater's theory of influence almost seventy years later, Shelley erases the boundary he draws between an external nature and an interior self at the moment he draws it:

> My own, my human mind . . . passively
> Now renders and receives fast influencings,
> Holding an unremitting interchange
> With the clear universe of things around. (37–40)

"Fantasy" isn't very private; it is connected to the "universe of things." Nor is the "universe of things" particularly metaphysical, especially when it is a function of "fast influencings." Even the primacy of the imaginative will is reduced to a structure of reception which it is the poet's call to organize. Neither imagination nor object is really primary, since each is a function of the other in their "interchange." Each needs the other to be what it is. Imagination puts the human subject in place by virtue of putting its very possibility at risk.

Shelley is not, as it turns out, talking about either a celestial or a natural sublime, with the cosmos functioning as an objective force in either scheme. No, like the Coleridge of "The Aeolian Harp" (1795), he is subject to a "universe," in both cases, "of things," indeed "of things around"—that is, of a secular rather than a metaphysical sublimity. The torrents that flow through him, the mountain, the poem (where are the lines that distinguish these presumable objects from one another anyway?) are those of history and influence, not of an inchoate sacred power, whether natural, philosophical, or religious. The presumably absolute solipsism that follows on the poem's presumable—and now discredited—objectivism is no more solipsistic than its Platonic idealism is genuinely objective. The poet's consciousness is rendered secondary, offering up instead a structural vision of the poet's unconscious ("passively") as both composer and receiver, receiver and compos(t)er. Like Bloom's or Emerson's, Shelley's is a theory of influence that regards the poet's oracularity as sieve and receptacle of historical overdetermination. Influence is no less, and no more, than a wealth of overdetermination. The poet is not, strictly speaking, a person, although only a person can be a poet. "Passively," hyperbolic as it is, represses altogether the active dimension of the process, but since its activity is also largely unconscious, it is an extraordinarily frank reassessment of the poet's relation to influence and a strong representation of what poetic strength involves.

The ironic result of this "interchange" is, however, Shelley's vision of Mont Blanc as objectified nature and of his own voice and imagination as autonomous. This is the poem's achievement, but it is an imaginative one, in neither case the record of a fact beheld. "The wilderness," says Shelley, has a "mysterious tongue" (76)—one is reminded of Jack London's *Call of the Wild* (1903)—although the sermons Shelley finds in stones have already been put there by imagination, just as the mountain has afforded imagination a place to roam. Imagination is not personal; it is a dynamic of "interchange," not between empirical subject and empirical object (as with Freud's primal scene, there is no genuinely primal scene here), but between the "torrents" of historical influence and an imagination that acts as a receptacle for it.

By the fourth section of the poem, Shelley is ready to describe the epistemology of his tropes in astonishingly precise detail, once again intimating Pater:

All things that move and breathe with toil and sound
Are born and die; revolve, subside, and swell. (94–95)

What this visionary site shows is the coming together and the dissolution of form as such. Indeed, there is no such thing as form as

such, since to distinguish form is to have acknowledged and ac-
cepted "interchange" with a system and history of signification that
have already organized subject and object in relation to one another.
And yet the ironic result of all this is nonetheless the keeping of the
faith that, yes, "[p]ower dwells apart"(96) from all things, "[r]emote,
serene, and inaccessible" (97), the latter one of language's most familiar tropes for placing something beyond place as a way, paradoxically, of placing it in the first place. If "the Sun" created "in scorn
of mortal power" (103), it is, however, no wonder that its creation
looks very like the products of mortality or the "universe of things,"
of people and their history: "dome, pyramid, and pinnacle, / A city
of death"—all cities are—"distinct with many a tower / And wall
impregnable" (105–6). But the poet refines his tune: this is "not a
city," he says, "but a flood of ruin" (107). Is it a fugitive or negative
cosmic power that Shelley is bent on mourning? Or is it the ability
to mourn that is itself part of the yield of the poem? With no small
irony, the "waste" (112) that this "flood of ruin" becomes is not a
wild sublime but a way of producing a difference between imagination and what is beyond it. The "waste" has, after all, "overthrown /
The limits of the dead and living world, / Never to be reclaimed," "a
dwelling-place / Of insects" (112–15). The establishment of these
"limits" or boundaries by overthrowing them is the poem's own
imaginative achievement, its way of seeing beyond time as a function of time's frustrations.

Now the structure of the fifth and final section of the poem is
clear. Its conclusion is almost entirely preoccupied with a reassertion
of just that primevality that Mont Blanc has been shown not to
possess throughout the earlier sections of the poem. The poem's
achieved myth of a given mountain or nature is precisely what it
tries to celebrate as it tries to close. "The power is there" (127), says
the poet, but he produces presence ("the power") by absence
("there"). By its lack, the "secret Strength of things" (139) throws
into question the very "Strength" the poem now seems to be cele-
brating. This is not a genuinely "secret Strength," but only a "secret
Strength of things / Which governs thought, and to the infinite
dome / Of Heaven is as a law" (139–41). It "governs thought," not the
world, and "is as"—"as"—"a law." If it "inhabits thee" (141)—the
mountain itself—it inhabits the mountain not as such but as an

achieved belief on our part. The Platonic or natural otherness of Mont Blanc is in fact, and quite ironically, the result of its ability to function as a reminder of the very strength of the "things"—the history and secularity, the mythologies of meaning, the towers and pyramids—to which it is, as a sublime site, presumably opposed. It is the strength of "things" that is the poem's real and awful discovery: the "things" that govern thought and that make the domes of a place in the imagination called "Heaven." It is this sad "secret" that puts in place its "Strength," not, alas, the "Strength" that puts into place the "secret." The poem constructs a loop.

Shelley's curious question at the end of the poem isn't so curious after all. "What were thou," he asks his subject mountain, "if to the human mind's imaginings / Silence and solitude were vacancy?" (142–44). The fear is that the "silence and solitude" really signify nothing at all. Indeed, Shelley is even willing to concede that meaning comes from "the human mind's imaginings" rather than from unmediated cosmic sources, so that what he really fears, finally, is weak or absent imagination rather than an absent world. The world is always absent. It is poets who fill it. The presumable givenness of the poet's voice is, of course, also subject to the same perils as are its objects. If the mountain emerges as a function of the poet's incantatory speech, the poet's incantatory speech likewise emerges as a function of the mountain it puts in place and the mythologies of meaning that help him to do so. The poet's voice vouchsafes its own natural expressiveness by virtue of the sublime object of ideology that its praxis stabilizes. Subjects and objects alike need each other to be what they are. Even the proper name Mont Blanc ironically evacuates its own propriety as a signifier, since what it names is, in almost postmodern fashion, *blanc*, blank, white. The stability of space and imagination alike gives way in "Mont Blanc" to a meditation on the politics of form. To see the horizon, not of the real but of form as such, is what kicks the real into what transitory yet strangely overwhelming sense it has. Nature is a myth, and the religion of nature that Romantic imagination bequeaths—that of a redemptive realm beyond culture—is, with some irony, one of culture's most durable achievements. "Poets," says Shelley at the close of *The Defense of Poetry* (1821), "are the unacknowledged legislators of the world."

HOW DOES THE FIGURE of the cowboy emerge out of Shelley? How indeed. "These horseback dandies," writes Zeese Papanikolas in *Trickster in the Land of Dreams*—the tropes are telling—"are servants of an ideology that had been imported to the West whole" (1995, 74). Romanticism's pop spawn included Walter Scott, and Scott's included James Fenimore Cooper. By all accounts, Cooper's Leatherstocking precedes and prefigures the cowboy as Western hero, although as a figure in his own right the cowboy was not mythologized as such, according to Henry Nash Smith, until Buffalo Bill became the darling of the Eastern press in the 1870s (1950, 123). As the nineteenth century wore on, writes Don Russell in his foreword to Cody's autobiography, a book originally published in 1879, Fenimore Cooper's "woodland" heroes "faded out," and the "tengallon hat and decorated chaps" faded in (1978, xvii). Buffalo Bill's life and legend present the characteristic features of the cowboy in particular and the West in general: an outrageous collapsing of fact into fiction and the conviction that real experience is played out in the terms of myth. The cowboy hides the machinery of his manner by exposing it. By insisting that the fantastic is true, the boundary or difference between fact and fiction is secured by its apparent transgression. The cowboy is realist and fantasist at once. The international fame of Cody's famous Wild West Show later in his career— it began in 1883 and had its final performance in 1913, the year the Woolworth Building was completed—adds, of course, to the problematic relation between fact and fiction in Western mythology, especially the prescient postmodernism of Cody's showmanship. Did his performance of himself represent his past experiences, or did it simply repeat them?

The rhetoric of Buffalo Bill's autobiography resembles the hyperbole of the dime novels, some penned by his friend Ned Buntline, and, later on, the Hollywood films that, like the Wild West Show, came after his own exploits. It is, however, also obvious from his autobiography that, in Cody's own mind—or at least in that larger or smaller part of it that he is willing to share with us—the later renditions of his experience don't just represent his recall of the facts of his life; they recapitulate them. Cody's birth is, in his own words, a *"début* upon the world's stage" (1879, 17), and his temperament that of a "restless, roaming spirit" (93). Cowboys, he says, have "huge pistols and knives in their belts" and wear "large broad-rimmed hats" (28); Indians come "dashing up, lashing their horses," which are as a rule "panting and blowing" (185); and, of course, "bull whips . . . crack" "like rifle shots" (64). "The life and adventures of Hon. William F. Cody," writes his publisher, Frank E. Bliss, in the introduction to the book's first edition, "reads [sic] more like romance than reality" (v). But, says Bliss, "[t]here is no humbug or braggadocio about Buffalo Bill. . . . [H]is reputation has been earned honestly and by hard work" (v). And part of his honesty, like Ben Franklin's, is that he is duty-bound not to lie about the fact that his life was from the start full of the stuff of legend.

Like Cody's autobiography, his sister Helen's later account of his life and exploits, published in 1899—a book sold by Indian hawkers as a promotion gimmick before performances of the Wild West Show—has an astonishingly regular rhetorical feature, too: an insistence on the difference between fact and fiction even as the difference is being undone. Both Codys are "faithful," in Bill's words (1879, 71), "veracious," in Helen's (Wetmore 1899, xv). "Embarrassed with riches of fact," writes Helen in her own preface, "I have had no thought of fiction" (xvi). And yet, she says, pressured by fact, "everything" is "animation" (33). Helen's biblical tropes alternate with Shelleyan ones in this "actual history of the West" (241). Her brother's life is one of "prophecy" (3), and his fancy "bounded by the hazy rim where plain and sky converge" (33). And yet "we found ourselves out of Eden," she confesses, "and in the desert that surrounded it" (229); the West is "one vast, untenanted waste" (176). Nonetheless—for her honesty, too, is rigorous—the mountains have, like Mont Blanc, "the appearance of a castle, with towers, turrets, bastions, and balconies" (236); "Pike's Peak lifts its snowy head to heaven" (290).

From what imaginative source or practice does the Codys' mythological impulse derive? Too regular to be arbitrary and too grand in structure and trope to be merely a family affair, Bill and Helen alike participate in a larger habit of American mind established and disseminated by the Romantic prophet Emerson. As Hermione Lee reminds us in her biography of Willa Cather, paraphrasing Cather's letter to a friend from New Mexico in 1912, the properly "self-educated Westerner," as she puts it, "read his bound copy of Emerson *all the time*" (1989, 87–88; Lee's italics). Before examining in some detail the ways in which Western history and Western mythology characteristically deny Emerson even as they are enabled by him, let us examine Emerson himself to see what the nature of the enablement is.

Shelley counts Emerson as family, of course, his outpost of progress, as it were, and a canonical figure in his own right, wonderfully positioned within a torrent of influences whose overdeterminations he manages to organize in texts so semiotically porous that they have produced almost endless schools of misreading. In 1836, the year he published *Nature,* Emerson was already as much a recipient of Western influence as he was a projectionist of the mythology of self-reliance that helped to gird Westward expansion. Ann Douglas calls him "a middle-man of history," an inheritor of Shelley and Cooper who even shook hands with Horace Greeley on a lecture trip to New York in 1842 (1977, 139, 336). As a good Virgilian writer responding to the influences around him, Emerson formalizes the mythology of expansion, both inside the mind and outside, in real space. In the process (a process that includes his own reception), he—"he"—stabilizes a tradition of belief and gives it its best expression. What is its technology?

Pure vacancy is not what Emerson had in mind when he called himself a "transparent eyeball" (1836, 24). It is a hyperbolic response to Shelley's unencouraging option of the vacant eye and also its primary Americanization. Like Shelley, Emerson is both the maker and the unmaker of boundaries and frontiers. To the poet, says Emerson, speaking of himself as well as of Shakespeare in *Nature,* "the refractory world is ductile and flexible; he invests dusts and stones with humanity, and makes them the words of the Reason" (44). "The Imagination may be defined to be the use which the Reason makes of the material world" (44). This is Emerson's visionary pragmatism, his "imperial muse," as he puts it (44), and one with a good future in real estate.

In fact, it is the unnamed image of the American West that looms up in the images of space and expansion that Emerson uses to describe the authority of a poet like Shakespeare:

> Shakespeare possesses the power of subordinating nature for the purposes of expression. . . . [He] tosses the creation like a bauble from hand to hand, and uses it to embody any caprice of thought that is uppermost in his mind. The remotest spaces of nature are visited, and the farthest sundered things are brought together, by a subtle spiri-

tual connection. We are made aware that magnitude of material things is relative, and all objects shrink and expand to serve the passion of the poet. (44)

The ironic image of expansion—of a subordinated creation—well describes the nature of poetic or imaginative power over a presumably blank (or *blanc*) material world, a world whose size is a paradoxical function of a large imagination's ability to seize it. Like boundaries in Shelley's "Mont Blanc," those of the "real" West, we should remember, kept changing, too: the frontier line moved ever westward over the course of the nineteenth century until Frederick Jackson Turner proclaimed it closed in 1893. As it was for the European colonizers beforehand, the West was never a literal place; the boundaries kept changing because an objective correlative had constantly to be found for a place of and in the imagination that materialized in the New World. It is hardly surprising for a polity to be founded upon a set of religious principles that had "lost its transitive reference," as Smith puts it (1950, 217), the price of—and the goad for—the fullness to which it, typologically at least, tried always to return; even Smith's remark is structured rhetorically as a Christian lament. In "Experience," in 1844, Emerson says the word "West" overtly, although its status as metaphor is left open: "I am ready to die out of nature," he says, "and be born again into this new yet unapproachable America I have found in the West" (267).

"The world," then, "exists to the soul," says Emerson in *Nature,* "to satisfy the desire of beauty" (31). But what is "the world" for Emerson? Is it a real empirical landscape to which the soul comes? Or does it come already made, a vault of influence? Wishing to keep this latter process as far removed from his own equivalent, prophetic one, Emerson calls it a "transformation . . . hidden from us" (31). This process vouchsafes what is real to us by virtue of the social technologies that precede the individual's—or the poet's—birth. For Emerson, as for the explorers, this use of nature is "an ultimate end" (31). Indeed, "Nature subserves to man" (31). The result is, in a frank turnaround, our ability to see at last "the final cause of Nature" (31). The "final cause of nature" is, after all, Romantic imagination, which stirs a landscape into life, puts it there, navigably, in the first place. "Cause and effect are two sides of one fact" (174), he says in "Circles" (1841, 184). He even gives us a good dose of Orientalist imagery in the process: for savages, language is an "immediate dependence . . . upon nature" (33) rather than the other way around, the latter—the dependence of nature upon language—the kind of attitude white settlers had, and would have, as they moved farther West. "Savages" are part of nature, not part of humanity. That's why they work so well as metaphors in Emerson's prose, just as the Alps do in Shelley's poem.

"The laws of moral nature"—of the American sublime, for example—"answer to those of matter as face to face in a glass" (1836, 34). The proleptic Lacanian wit (and the shared battle against the New Testament even as both Emerson and Lacan write one) suggests that what moral nature sees is, as Emerson has already plainly put it, its own image stamped upon a presumable object world that would not itself exist without the imagination of mythology and the mythology of imagination. Joseph Smith, the Mormon pioneer, stamps the object world literally, reducing Emerson's own mild romance with Muhammed as both Old and New Testament reviser by simply inventing a new religion. The joke, however, is that this is in any case how the world is always stirred into life. Even "savages converse in figures" (33). "Life is our dictionary" (71), says Emerson in *The American Scholar* (1837), not just because the world is mythologically produced ("The world is his who can see through its pretension" [75]), but also because—and this is why it works—even the dictionary is of our own making.

"We animate what we can," says the franker Emerson of "Experience," "and we see only what we animate" (257). In fact, this contention leads to a famous pronouncement: "The world is all outside. It has no inside" (263). Then again, "there is no outside," he says in "Circles," feeling his own strength rise, "no inclosing wall, no circumference to us" (170). This amounts to saying that there is neither outside nor inside, since each comes into being, as it were, only in relation to the other. The West is ungraspable by definition. There is nothing after all to capture, only a horizon to be infinitely expanded and a world to be made more fluid, supple, flexible. Moreover, the world's expansiveness induces a greater depth in the subject, by reflexive necessity. The same paradox structures the poet, too, who becomes in this formulation not a person but a function or an agency, even if only a person can be a poet. History and the poet make one another, much as subjects and objects do.

Indeed, throughout his career, Emerson's theory of the poet resembles Shelley's. Emerson is, of course, as much a function of influence as he is a progenitor of it, reflexively enacting his own (self-)representation. "All I know," he says in "Experience," echoing Shelley's "passively," "is reception" (272). Boon victim of such an influx of historical determination—Emerson's deistic vocabulary requires him to call this secular afflatus the famous "waves of God" (176) in "Circles"—Emerson also learns from it, much as Shelley learns to convert imagination and vacancy into a dialectic of presence and absence. Aswim in this sea of waves, Emerson, is, like Shelley himself, all reception. "The Universe is the externalization of the soul" (227), he says in "The Poet" (1844), although it is also the other way around. Externalization is even too sharp a word to describe the process. Externalization and interiorization are, to use Saussure's figure, two sides of the same sheet of paper, or, to use Emerson's own figure, two sides of the same coin. All symbols are fluxional; all language is rhetorically, not empirically, vehicular and transitive (237), requiring referents to serve its execution. Given this flux, the real imaginative precondition for the poet, "the sayer, the namer" (224), is one that starts the imagination into this kind of imperial musing as a defense against the constitutive instability of language that it manages to—that it is designed to—override.

The authority of the poet comes not from a personal Puritan wellspring of divine spirit but from just the opposite: a surrender of personality, of precisely one's personal will, and an openness instead to those waves of God whose name in our own age is historical overdetermination or the ravages of tradition. As with Shelley, nature, like the universe, is also a nature of "things": "beside his privacy of power as an individual . . . there is a great public power on which [the poet] can draw, by unlocking at all risks his human doors, and suffering the ethereal tides to roll and circulate through him; then he is caught up into the life of the Universe, his speech is thunder, his thought is law, and his words are universally intelligible" (233). In a reflexive example of his argument, Emerson's own rhetoric is itself a sea of often perilous discrepancies between a religious vocabulary and a historicist one. Despite the use of words such as "celestial," Emerson's is, like Shelley's, a secular vision and one that invokes "a great public power," the real nature of the "tides" that "roll and circulate" through us by virtue of historical usage. The

poet takes on authority by organizing a stance out of the compo-
nents of this vortex of prior mythological and poetic determination,
as a function of it rather than of himself or herself alone, navigating
its tides or, in the Coleridgean metaphor for influence, its winds. The
poet can influence in turn by restructuring this heritage of forms all
over again. The poet is a container or receptacle, to use Pater's
phrase, and is as much a function of determination as landscape or
world is a function of the poet's mythographical success in outstrip-
ping those determinations, handling their points of connection in a
new way. History and the poet make one another.

What are the consequences and lessons of this view of things?
"Every ship is a romantic object," says a Magellanesque Emerson in
"Experience," "except that we sail in" (255). In other words, the
world has meaning to the extent that it is mythologized, but the
price of one's sense of reality is that one's own mythological situation
must be repressed. Death, says Emerson, is the only "reality that will
not dodge" (257), even while the rest of life is nothing but dodg-
ing—Dodge City, if you will. Our sense of life, as Emerson puts it
here, is "a train of moods"—one sees the railways being built; "a
string of beads" (257)—one sees San Francisco 130 years later. "We
animate what we can," says Emerson, "and we see only what we animate" (257), an observation refreshingly paganlike in its expansiveness but dauntingly monotheistic when push comes to shove. "Nature and books" alike, he concludes, "belong to the eyes that see
them" (257). Emerson's agon with Shelley is of the same order as the
American sublime's agon with Europe at large. "Gladly we would
anchor," says Emerson, promoting his sea imagery, "but the anchor-
age is quicksand" (259), even the Shelleyan sands of the Painted
Desert, as it were, to come. This, alas, is why the hegemony of
mythology is necessary, at least to the culture on the practicing end
of it. "Life itself is a mixture of power and form" (261), and the two
together produce a mythos of the real that one can live in, through,
and with. As if to solve the presumable conflict between his solipsism and his communitarianism, Emerson simply makes the external
a function of internal poetic or imaginative investments—beliefs
and mythologies when they become cultural consensus, conscious
and assumptive alike. There is neither outside nor inside because
both are organized in relation to one another, forming a loop or a

crossing. Hence the dominion of mythological imagination is both necessary and inevitable. This is Emerson's "[p]ractical power" (274).

GIVEN EMERSON'S IMAGINATIVE SWAY, it is not surprising that the customary—and Emersonian—lament of traditional Western historians is that Easterners first painted the West in the colors of European, that is to say Romantic, influence. It is, of course, a defensive lament—a denial—and a wider version of the denial of fiction in the name of fact practiced by the Codys. To put it frankly, Western historiographers as a rule repress the link between an enabling Emersonian Romanticism and the deep structure, as the old saying goes, of the West's mythification. "The East," writes R. E. Lee, "controlled the language by which the West could define itself" (1966, 1). "The metaphors of Western histories," in Martin Bucco's words, "are more poetic than scientific" (1984, 52). Hence the relation between Emerson and the West itself emerges silently and negatively against a tradition of Western studies that, in the past at least, has failed to mention Emerson very much at all, usually invoking Thoreau in his place whenever logic requires a nod East.

As both life and art, the West tends to resist (and thus to prove) the effectiveness of the New England self-reliance that ironically empowers it. What the West as an institution necessarily represses, both on the ground and in literal texts, is its own historically enabling Romanticism—to disguise its imperialism pragmatically and to maintain its originality imaginatively. Praising the Western landscape for its uniqueness, the explorer Frémont regularly waxes almost argumentatively transcendental in his diary, even indulging in a Shelleyan occupatio at the very moment that he recalls the American difference from High Romanticism: "Though these snow mountains are not the Alps," he writes of the Northwest in 1843, "they have their own character of grandeur and magnificence, and will doubtless," he says without conscious irony, "find pens and pencils to do them justice" (1843, 255). If Emerson himself often represses the proper name of the West even as he describes and legitimates it as a combined imaginative and pragmatic invention, the West itself, as both a discourse of life and of letters, tends as a rule to obscure in its own turn the mythology of self-reliance upon which the cowboy or Westerner is propped. The denial of Emerson is structured by a reduced version of Emerson's own habit of mind.

Even the Turner thesis of 1893 is itself a moment within the tradition it seeks to portray, although its figures of speech sometimes make it seem momentarily self-conscious. Without naming names, Turner blurts out in murky metaphors—and with a remarkable frankness—that a certain predetermination emanating from "an intellectual stream [of] New England sources," as he puts it, "fertilized the West" (1893, 36). "The United States lies like a huge page in the history of society," he says, and "this page is a palimpsest" (11). "There is not," as he puts it at the essay's close, *"tabula rasa"* (38). Textualizing the frontier undoes its primacy, and the additional quality of its being a palimpsest (even a tabula rasa is, properly speaking, a scraped slate, not a clean one) clarifies some of the reasons: a precedent discourse—Emerson's, for example—seems always to have put the meaningful object in place beforehand. The power of art's ironically prefigurative relation to life remains consistent even as the expanding boundaries of the West do not.

These ironies were not, however, lost on the West as a practice. Killing Indians, murdering Asian workers, driving women to madness—only a notion, sometimes a great one, of the West as mythically endowed with echoes of biblical promise could account for the willful and presumably guiltless perpetration of massacres and exploitations whose representation preoccupies the work of Richard Slotkin (1973, 1985, 1992). Slotkin's revisionary, realist reading explains why the mythic reading was necessary in the first place—to cover, no, to render the violence invisible, in Ralph Ellison's sense of the term, under the mystification of an ideal. The West, both as experience and as the abstract idea of wild, unlimited space, presumably had no models in the rhetoric of imagination that as a rule accompanied both its representation and its various vernaculars. The pretense of the West as Christian garden is likely the most innocuous of the reductions and literalizations of the historical materiality of Emerson's vision (and one overturned by Helen Cody's "out of Eden"), but it is nonetheless another defensive and compensatory instance of how the rhetoricity behind Westward expansion had to be eternalized in order not to be noticed (for an influential reading, see Marx 1964; for a catalog of the naturalizations, see Allmendinger 1992, 40).

The traditional repression of Emerson has as its plainest symptom the discourse of Western realism, both as an aesthetic practice and as a way of life. Western realism, whether as a political or a literary discourse, treats, to use Pater's phrase, colored glass as if it were clear. The realism of the Westerner is his or her most Emersonian characteristic. It bespeaks a self-reliance born of absolute (self-)assumption, the most durable kind of realism there is (see Fender 1981, 83, 118). Perhaps, then, Emerson's greatest success is the reaction against him and all he represents by the West he helped to invent—a reaction not only against the East in the name of an emergent and still vivid regionalism, but also a decidedly literary reaction, one couched in the direct terms of a realism that upbraids the Romanticism of Easterners.

Western historiography is not, however, all repression. There are, for example, traditional accounts of the link between Emerson and the West—by Easterners. Well before F. O. Matthiessen's *American Renaissance* invents American studies in 1941, Lewis Mumford's remarkable book *The Golden Day* (1926) makes it plain that "the pioneer," as Mumford puts it, "existed in the European mind before he made his appearance here" (47). Mumford connects Western expansion with High Romanticism (53) and dubs Emerson "the leader" of this connection (94). Matthiessen, too, acknowledges the relation between Emerson and High Romanticism (1941, 133 ff.), as do R. W. B. Lewis in 1955, Edwin Fussell in 1965, and G. Edward White in 1968. Robert Weisbuch, in a more recent study (1986), shows in great detail what the nature of the British burden was for the American writer, particularly the influence of Romanticism.

Weisbuch's approach to American writing coincides with a new and welcome tendency among Western historians over the last twenty years, an approach that culminates in the New Western History. A powerful and newly self-conscious attempt to move beyond repression on Western ground itself, it shows that even the West of Westerners is always a twice-told tale. "In the years since 1970," writes John Cawelti in the introduction to the second edition (1984) of his decisive study, *Six-Gun Mystique* (1970), "the myth has become increasingly attenuated" (11). New Western History has its official beginning with the publication in 1987 of Patricia Nelson Limerick's *The Legacy of Conquest: The Unbroken Past of the American West*, although critics and historiographers from Jay Gurian (1975) to Annette Kolodny (1984) already show that the actual experience of the West is as a rule cast in the mythologies that supposedly only followed it or that it somehow left behind. Western experience is, to put it simply, one of "mediated realities," to use Carol Fairbanks's phrase in *Prairie Women* (1986, 25; see also Fender 1981; Walker 1981; Udall 1990; and Allmendinger 1992).

Self-named, New Western History calls itself, with some irony, "a new historiographical frontier" (Nash and Etulain 1989, 1). It reassesses the cultural history of Westward expansion and its ideological grounding, especially—and at last—in the terms of the American mythologies developed by Eastern Romantic writers earlier in the nineteenth century. New Western History is, inevitably, "'a story about stories,'" as James R. Grossman puts it, describing an exhibtion at the Newberry Library marking the joint appearance of Buffalo Bill and Frederick Jackson Turner in Chicago a hundred years before (1994, 2). Essay collections such as *Desert, Garden, Margin, Range* (Heyne 1992) show in detail the hitherto repressed mythological motivation in representations of the frontier from Cooper and Daniel Boone—and Emerson—to contemporary writing (Mary Lawlor even demonstrates how the crossings of fiction and authenticity in the history of Boone are structurally identical with those we have seen at work in the history of Buffalo Bill [1992, 29 ff.]). Limerick's collection *Trails* (Limerick et al. 1991) similarly charts the ideological structures that both stimulated and contained Westward expansion from the 1880s into the twentieth century. The work of Harold Simonson was the exception and is now the exemplum, beginning in 1970 with *The Closed Frontier,* a remarkable reading of the frontier as an enactment of Emersonianism and its own prior determinations in American Puritanism, and elaborating the premise with *Radical Discontinuities* (1983) and *Beyond the Frontier* (1989), the latter explicitly linking Western expansion with Eastern writers such as Emerson, Whitman, and Melville.

In both exaggerated and understated ways, American fiction itself has often provided the kind of representation of Westernism appropriate to it under the strictures by which the West's emergence as place and as discourse has been determined. Stephen Crane's enduring respectability as a writer, for example, is likely the result of his ready affection for the mythic air of both his narrative protocols and the conventions of the West that they represent. "The Bride Comes to Yellow Sky" (1897) is a good case in point. More than seventy years later on, Ishmael Reed takes similar conventions for his subject in *Yellow Back Radio Broke-Down* (1969) but narrates instead the thick undertow of their assumptions. It is Mark Twain, of course, as Tony Tanner long ago pointed out (1965), who first solves the problem of a self-conscious representation of the West by inventing what Stephen Fender calls the "double style" (1981, 14) characteristic of frontier writing, a style that is at once vivid and true, realist while also reflexive or self-aware (see also Tanner 1965, 129). Like Whitman, or like Wordsworth, Twain treats vernacular not as a proof of presence but as a lived mythology that grants character identity by virtue of its measurable swerves from rule. Indeed, if we read history as literature, then Slotkin's historical realism is a narrative response to the Turner tradition of Romantic naturalism. In Frank Norris's *McTeague* (1899), of course, the narrator—the book's real presence—skillfully oscillates between a terse realism and a more plainly Romantic mode of prophecy, becoming, finally, a prophet of the mundane. The landscape of the West resolves the two in the book's terrifying climax.

As it turns out, the same kind of double structure that attends the history of the West also attends the history of Emerson's own critical reception and clarifies what they share more exactly. Ever since David B. Davis academicized the study of the cowboy in 1954 with his essay "Ten-Gallon Hero," the paradox of the loner or outlaw who toils for the group has baffled and enthralled historians of the frontier. Similarly, the enduring state of Emerson criticism revolves around an argument as to whether Emerson is a prophet of the ego or a pragmatic collectivist (see, for example, Levin 1975), a debate structured on the one hand by Emerson's egotistical sublime and, on the other, by the pragmatic, collectivist Emerson discovered, for example, in Stanley Cavell's readings of Emerson in recent years (1988, 1989, 1990). The argument is easily solved by noting that it is precisely the bifurcated rhetoric within Emerson himself that makes his texts—like Shelley's, or like Pater's to come—functions of their own internal dissonances. Like Shelley, Emerson transgresses his own soul language with the language of historicity, replacing one with the other in a regular rhetorical rhythm. We should note, too, that the irony of Emerson's own influence is that the cult of the individual legitimized by texts such as "Self-Reliance" has itself, paradoxically, become a social myth. Our common life is about our individuality. Quentin Anderson's imperial self (1971) is as reductive in a cowboyish way as is a reading seeking only Emerson's collectivism (see, for example, West 1989). Neither alone responds sufficiently to Emerson's constitutive asymmetries.

The contradictions that structure Emerson are the same contradictions or oppositions that structure the mythology of the cowboy that both precedes and follows him. The cowboy acts out the paradox at the center, as it were, of Emerson himself: the solitary who labors for the ironic sake of community. This tension is already at work in Leatherstocking (both Boone and Davy Crockett eventually ran for Congress) and, in a different key, in late-century heroes of the Farther West like the dandy Bat Masterson and the gunslinger novelist Buntline. This shared paradox in the history of both Emerson studies and the history of the cowboy is not, of course, a problem to be solved but, like Shelley's "Mont Blanc" or Emerson's essays, a familiar site, that of the law and its transgression. The crossing passage back and forth between the two produces the boundary between them, whether of Mont Blanc as form as such, or of the West and the line it draws between civilization and nature. That Europe and the East provide the West with the languages it needed to express its sublime originality is an overwhelmingly reflexive instance of the paradox of reciprocity that cowboy wisdom wishes as an enabling rule to repress. It is, however, also a reduced version of the same rhetorical feint that characterizes both Emerson's writing and Shelley's—the technical illusion of natural things that are in fact made by culture. This is the empowering strategy that Emerson and Shelley share, a crossing over into landscape by means of imaginative machinery whose role in the process is typically denied.

3

INFLUENCE and ORIGINALITY
in BLUES TRADITION

The sound of urban or electric blues is, as we all know, uncanny, in Freud's sense of the word—something at once strange and familiar. Hence its defining paradox—a witting confusion of the terms of the struggles it presumably represents, the struggles between country and city, youth and age, soul and machine, freedom and bondage, nature and culture. While the route of jazz from Armstrong to swing documents a successful transit of country blues to classic or city blues, electric blues is almost a step backward even though, like rhythm and blues, it follows classic blues chronologically: electric blues is a ferocious meditation on the difference between country and city itself and a willful undoing of the very urbanity that jazz by definition achieves. It focuses on the construction of the relation between country and city rather than on the relation itself. No mere expressive mode, electric blues is a highly critical or reflexive mode that doesn't just register a crossing from country to city but performs a crossing back, a movement in reverse. The elegance of the Southern city bluesmen may contrast with the blasted agedness of their Chicago counterparts—the finish of T-Bone Walker of Houston, say, as distinct from the cragginess of Howlin' Wolf—but in both cases the decidedly mannered result is testimony to a discovery of form rather than a discovery of directness. These are not moral terms but categorical ones. Instead of a line of progress from country to city, electric blues is a loop or crossing over that is always in both places at once. It also reflects the new learnedness that invades blues tradition as a whole after swing, a tradition now sufficiently dense with precedent to cause the kinds of self-consciousness and anxiety with which we are familiar, say, in bop or, later on, in Coltrane to emerge as well in an electric blues mode whose achieved simplicity we too often misread as plain frankness. Electric blues also prefigures the fate of our paradigm in rock and roll as a whole, already rehearsing in the mid-1940s the way in which the electric and the acoustic will come to signal the difference between country and city, and the way in which electric instruments will allow rock and roll to reimagine jazz itself—an acoustic music—as an earlier form and so clear a new and distinct space for its own exertions.

Muddy Waters is, of course, the pioneer example of the bluesman who moved North from the South, from the Delta to Chicago, from acoustic guitar to electric, from the country to the city. A juke-joint performer in Mississippi, Waters left for Chicago in 1943. In 1944, writes Robert Palmer, he bought his first electric guitar, and the band he eventually put together was, in Palmer's words, "the first important electric band" (1981, 15, 16; see also Guralnick 1971, 60, 64 ff.). Chicago bluesmen, simply put, "electrified the Delta blues" (Barlow 1989, 331), often imitating the jump sound of Louis Jordan's band in the process (Palmer 1981, 221). Here country and city structure what is, on the one hand, the rather straightforward use of city technology to transform a rural sound into an urban one. On the other hand, however, the transformation has the effect of loosening the stability of the distinctions that ordinarily structure the difference between country and city itself. What divides rude and elegant, expression and sophistication? Electric blues is a surpassing inquiry into the terms of the sublime.

What, you may ask, listening to Waters sing, is the nature of that voice? Why does its huskiness, its thick, debauched quality, strike you so? Not because of its vaunted naturalness or primitivism. It is the dire historicity of Waters's voice that really affects us, however grave the pleasure is. Waters's originality is a function of his voice's struggle with the burdens of influence behind it, chief among them his own prior career as an acoustic bluesman, a struggle that is not so much resolved as it is held in suspension. Like country and city, influence and originality are the poles of a single paradigm, and Waters's voice, like his own history, crosses over endlessly between the two. When he sings, as he often does, of lost country pleasures from the heights of Chicago—on "I Feel Like Going Home" (1948), "Southbound Train" (1959), or "My Home Is in the Delta" (1963)—it is no act of simple nostalgia but a sharpening of the tensions that structure him. He acknowledges the sources of his own originality in influences that have been left behind, including, with less regret than delight, his own less revisionary role in blues history as a Delta performer. Indeed, the ruined quality of blues voice as such—Waters's or Armstrong's or Blind Lemon Jefferson's—results from a tradition of use whose burden is what bristles in its customary grain, turns it into the very instrumentality or secondariness to which it is normally, presumably, opposed.

But while this tendency or effect is, of course, present in Armstrong and in country blues alike, it is the use of electric that in Waters's case—and in electric blues as a whole—pushes the effect into a qualitatively different aesthetic space. This new sound undoes the customary relation between voice and instrument far more overtly and dangerously than jazz and acoustic blues do and already highlights the rich and troubled relation between voice and instrument that the British blues bands of the 1960s and 1970s exploit more than any other device available to them to get a psychedelic sound. Thus Chicago blues, Waters in particular, is really the best way of showing our problematic at work in both a specific and an institutional way in those postwar years that saw the emergence of rock and roll music as a swerve from swing. Chicago blues is a microcosm of our paradigm, since it is the belated reconstruction or re-membering of a country rawness based, ironically, upon electric technology, and amplified to manage in urban surroundings. Let us consider Waters in brief detail to see how these terms are elaborated.

Waters's earliest electric recordings for Chess between 1947 and early 1954 provide the best look at what the play between voice and electric guitar actively accomplishes and what protocols it establishes for the rock and roll future. Waters's voice characteristically moves between a cleanliness and a graininess that between them structure the same double effect produced by his guitar. Very often, too, voice and guitar trade qualities, as they do on "Train Fare Home Blues" (1948), the bottleneck scraping of the guitar chordings rivaling the desecrated voice in grain. At other times, voice and guitar are counterposed. Even when voice is relatively clean, as it is on "Mean Red Spider" (1948), "Flood" (1950), or "Long Distance Call" (where it is especially pure [1951]), Waters's guitar supersedes it in edge. Then again, guitar can be remarkably clean next to the relative haziness of voice, as it is on "Baby Please Don't Go" (1953), boosted, too, by Little Walter's doubling of Jimmy Rogers's second-guitar line on harmonica. Voice and guitar also double one another—on "Rollin' and Tumblin'" (1950), say, or "Still a Fool" (1951). On "Rolling Stone" (1950), guitar plays against itself, like two voices, while on "Little Geneva" (1949), the guitar solo sounds less like a guitar than like a flippy, temperamental voice. This exchangeability between voice and guitar breaks down our usual expectations as to the customarily stable relation between voice and instrument. Guitar may be jagged and voice pure, but the moment such stability is reached, the qualities are once again often reversed. The presumable relation between voice and instrument, especially the naturalness of voice next to the given artificiality of the instrument, is a relation whose coherence is as a rule put in jeopardy. With some irony, Delta blues, of course, is similar—Waters's own early acoustic recordings for Alan Lomax are plain evidence—but with the superaddition of electricity, the heightening of the difference also heightens the breakdown of the difference.

Blues voice, then, actually topples the very naturalness we ordinarily associate with it, constantly muddying the differences between voice and instrument, country and city, nature and culture, primary and secondary that we otherwise take for granted in its functioning. Natural privilege is, in one fell stroke, abolished. Here music's chief activity is riffing and grooving far more than it is the rue or joy of telling a story in operatic mode. Blues narrative is more strategic than that. Indeed, the difference between story and narration gets muddied by the blues, too, since the story line as a rule tells us nothing new (we always know it beforehand), while the relation between voice and guitar, by contrast, always dramatizes something very new indeed—the guitar's stunning laceration of voice, which is never lamented, never bewailed, never even commented upon, unless in the positive, by the singer or the audience. Voice is no longer counterposed ontologically to band or orchestra as it is in what may be called operatic humanism, where even gendered voices maintain a credible difference from one another, a difference that blues tradition also undoes by using falsetto, as Waters does. In blues tradition, voice and instrument are, in fact, the same in epistemological status. Pure as they may seem to be, the waters are always already muddy. Even the formal dialogue between singers and their guitars raises more questions about who is troped as what than it is designed to settle. A later rock band with a name like Creedence Clearwater Revival, however reasonable or not musically, reminds us of the impossible wish for the originality or the clarity of origins that no medium allows. The material in which the musician works is no more his or her own than the sculptor's marble.

As if to showcase these ironies, electric blues would have been impossible without the precedent of jazzman Charlie Christian in the Thirties, swingman and proto-bopper and the figure who turned electric guitar into a real and feasible improvisatory jazz instrument. "Who the hell wants to hear an electric guitar player?" asked Benny Goodman when John Hammond proposed Christian as a new member of his band in 1939 (Hammond 1977, 224). "With Christian," writes Ralph Ellison, "the guitar found its jazz voice" (1958, 240). T-Bone Walker in Houston, the father of electric blues guitar as we know it, is the circuit between Christian and Muddy Waters (Palmer 1981, 17), although a series of earlier guitarists, especially the early rockers of Texas swing bands, preceded Walker and Christian alike (see Palmer 1992). It was Christian, writes Gunther Schuller, who put guitar on a plane with the solo horn in jazz in the Thirties (1989, 571); it is not until after the war that the distinction between horn and guitar becomes an issue in its own right, once Christian's playing had spread its influence sufficiently to produce a cadre of disciples. "The usual droning saxophone section background to a vocal," notes Charles Keil of the new blues, "becomes superfluous if both electric bass and guitar are present" (1966, 68).

Nor is the negative relation of electric blues to bebop any more surprising than King Curtis's is; it also bespeaks a continuity. Like Jordanesque rhythm and blues or the early Ray Charles, electric blues is another major example of the alternatives to Parker that emerge simultaneously as swerves from swing. Walker emerges out of jazz, too, as a contraction, a curtailment of protobop swing guitar, a tradition he establishes that later leads through Eric Clapton. What remains shocking, however, is that electric blues guitar comes after and out of Charlie Christian, not the other way around; electric blues guitar is a belated reduction of Christian rather than Christian's being a refinement of the latter. Electric blues at large, and Chicago blues in particular, is a self-consciously retroactive primitivism that uses jazz techniques and electricity to rearticulate Delta blues. In the wake of swing come both the grandest sophistication that jazz had ever known—bop—and a belated return via electric to its earliest roots. The irony is extraordinary: jazz on the one hand grows more presumably cultured than ever with bop while, at the very same time, the presumable naturalness of country blues is being adapted to the electricity of urbanity. One is still tempted to call electric blues the cowboy, the country, and bop the dandy, the city. But then again, the blues is now electric, while Charlie Parker himself is a very heavy bluesman indeed. As usual, the poles exchange just as you put them in place. The fact that Southern city blues as a rule has a smoother, more urbane sound than northerly Chicago's is another example of the endless crossings back and forth.

Chuck Berry well exemplifies the continuity between the new urban blues and what we call rock and roll proper. Like Muddy Waters, he began his recording career with Chess Records, the preeminent Chicago blues label of the postwar years. It was Waters who, not surprisingly, put Berry in touch with Leonard and Phil Chess (Waters had signed with them in 1947); Berry signed a recording contract in 1955. As in Waters's music—despite the obvious differences—the dynamic between voice and instrument, country and city, nature and culture, horn and guitar is key. Berry reimagines this dynamic in an astonishingly new way that reveals his own decisive relation to swing, and that shows, too, how the opposition of voice and instrument has an equivalent in the opposition of horns and guitar.

Berry's jump guitar—for that is what it is—is really a swing horn section in a different technology. Country influence aside, the signature hop chordings have as their only real precursor and counterpart the jumping horn sections of swing orchestras, a fact reflected in Berry's own testimony that swing bands launched his desire to play music as a youngster, especially Tommy Dorsey's "Boogie Woogie" (Berry 1987, 25–26). Reacting to swing even more originally than Louis Jordan, he reimagines it through electric guitar instead of through saxophone. Rhythmically, after all, Berry plays over what is really a swing tempo, and his guitar inventiveness rides perfectly on top of it. Even harmonically, his signature riffs are those of a swing horn section transformed by a technological availability hitherto un-exploited. Rock and roll guitar is the swing horn section transistorized.

One has only to turn to "Johnny B. Goode" (1958) to see this transformation plainly. The guitar riffs, both at the tune's start and during the two solos (one in the middle and one at the end), are Basie-band horns reconceived on guitar. The song's focus is also shifted to the guitar by the lyrics, which have Berry urging on another guitarist in the tale he sings. Of course, with no small irony, the purity of Berry's voice contrasts with the metal of his instrument, a reversal in turn of the way his guitar absorbs the breath of the reed. There are as a rule (with a few exceptions such as "Nadine" [1964]) no horns at all on Berry's hits. This absence is decisive. Guitar replaces the horns at the center of the sound, a major moment in the very history of music and largely Chuck Berry's doing. Once again, but in another key, breath is turned into technology, nature into art. Much as horns transistorize voice in a jazz band, so guitar transistorizes horns in a rock and roll band (the shift from ska to reggae is the Jamaican version). Berry's is the originary rock and roll gesture, the taking to the limit of a deconstruction of the difference between acoustic and electric, country and city, nature and culture that structures the history of jazz and blues at large and that makes the history of rock and roll continuous with them both. It is also what empowers rock and roll in relation to them.

The structure at work in the new electric blues, early rock and roll, and Romanticism all alike, then, is one of crossing, or crossing over. Loops or crossings fashion boundaries between a presumably natural self and the world, between an inside and an outside, the timely and the belated, a landscape and an eye. What constitutes the difference, moment to moment, between human and machine, nature and culture, voice and instrument? Between primitive and sophisticated, originality and influence, country and city, cowboy and dandy? Are these questions testimony to alienation? Or are they representations of a series of necessities, questions that actually put in place the world whose coherence they doubt? What, after all, is common to cowboy and dandy, country and city alike? The posting of boundaries by means of their violation. Far from naturalizing anything, rock and roll tradition confuses the nature of the differences involved in order to explore the plasticity of form itself. The desire for self-expression in blues and rock and roll singing, for example, preconditionally collides with the wall or machine of upstart determinism that presumably inhibits or resists it. The strain produces it from the very start. The movement within rock and roll from Jerry Lee Lewis, say, to Robert Plant simply makes the difference more dramatic. Like Waters's self-revisionary reaction to his earlier country playing, the change to electric only sharpens the issue that is already there. Much as East and West, dandy and cowboy, inside and outside need each other as foils or counterparts, so, too, do voice and instrument, labor and machine, country and city. Like Shelley or Emerson, rock and roll takes its own enabling tensions as its thematic quarry.

Like jazz, rock and roll is the function of vexed relations, of agons with prior traditions. Customary claims for its spontaneity are denials of history. While electric makes the inevitability of influence a graphic precondition of sound in urban blues or in rock and roll itself, such inevitability is, of course, already at work in Armstrong. Like Waters's to come, or prefiguring Bob Dylan's because Dylan reimagines him and Waters alike, even Armstrong's voice is already a legacy of usages that testifies to the instrumentality rather than to the self-presence of voice; voice always comes from somewhere else, even when it seems to be one's own. Indeed, Armstrong's trumpet—his instrument—sounds, uncannily, purer than his voice. Voice is the ironic function of an instrumentality to which it is opposed. The divine essence represented by the purity of the soprano, say, in classical singing is the difference that jazz in the first instance undoes. Also behind Armstrong and the whole history of Dixieland is an agon with European pop forms, the polka of Central European immigrants in particular (on crossover within the sphere of polka's influence, see Greene 1992), and another with opera's own pop spawn, the European music hall. Jazz's originary and agonistic relation to European music proceeds, moreover, by means of its use of fugitive African sources as the only defense at first available with which to deflect the discourse of the oppressor. Forged amid contending tongues, the hybrid nature of American music is not, as the saying goes, the function of a pure origin, but the function of any series of overdetermined relations.

Oscar Wilde in America, 1882
(Corbis-Bettmann)

Kit Carson
(George Rinhart/Corbis-Bettmann)

Beau Brummell
(Corbis-Bettmann)

John Lennon and
Paul McCartney, London, 1967
(UPI/Corbis-Bettmann)

Mick Jagger, 1969
*(Express Newspapers/
Archive Photos)*

Brian Jones, c. 1967
(Popperfoto/Archive Photos)

Elvis Presley, Memphis, 1970
(UPI/Corbis-Bettmann)

Cab Calloway in
"Stormy Weather" (1943)
(Frank Driggs/Corbis-Bettmann)

Ray Charles, 1967
(UPI/Corbis-Bettmann)

Bob Dylan, 1976
(AP/Wide World Photos

Muddy Waters, 1979
(AP/Wide World Photos)

Earl Bostic
(AP/Wide
World Photos)

John Coltrane
*(AP/Wide World
Photos)*

Jimi Hendrix, 1967 *(Popperfoto/Archive Photos)*

Janis Joplin
(AP/Wide World Photos)

Patti Smith
*(AP/Wide
World Photos)*

McKinney's Cotton
Pickers, Detroit,
1929 *(Frank
Driggs/Archive
Photos)*

The Beau Brummels, c. 1965
(Frank Driggs/Archive Photos)

Beck
*(Reuters/Nitin Vadukul/
Archive Photos)*

Buffalo Bill poster, 1900
(Corbis-Bettmann)

Willa Cather *(Corbis-Bettmann)*

Louis Armstrong in
"Every Day's a Holiday" (1937)
(Metronome Collection/
Archive Photos)

Miles Davis
(Metronome Collection/Archive Photos)

4

the PSYCHEDELIC SUBLIME

Let us cast our gaze across the Atlantic, back to England.
It is just after the French Revolution, and not long after
the loss of the American colonies. Aristocracy is besieged. Its indif-
ference is beginning to fail as a style, or at least to be an inappropri-
ate response given the pressures of the age. It needs a prop, and
finds it in the figure of George "Beau" Brummell, the first famous
dandy. A ceremonial military officer attached to the court of George
III and a favorite of the Prince of Wales, Brummell retired from his
regiment in 1798 and took a house in London, spreading the influence of his languid manner and affected and elegant mode of dress
until debts ruined him in 1816. Ellen Moers, in her classic study *The
Dandy: From Brummell to Beerbohm* (1960), traces the roots of the
term *dandy* to a song that handsomely uniformed British soldiers
sang about the ragtag American troops during the Revolutionary
War (1960, 11–13). Everyone knows the song—"Yankee Doodle
Dandy." The term is thus "an ambiguous symbol" (13), as Moers
puts it, since it blurred the line between who was who at the very
moment that the dandy British trooper aimed it, with presumable
contempt, at his American counterpart.

The word's etymology recounts an even longer history of usage
and, as Moers's example suggests, systematically undoes any unitary
meaning it may seem to have. The first meaning of "dandy" is, of
course, the elegance affected by the likes of Brummell. This usage
dates from the period following Brummell's ascendancy (1813–19), although it derives from "Jack a Dandy," a Scottish border expression

of the late eighteenth century meaning a "swell." It is the troubled legacy of empire that emerges in the history of the word's additional meanings, both before and after Brummell's apparent monopoly on the term. In 1828, on the island of St. Thomas, "English Negroes," so the *Oxford English Dictionary* tells us, used the term "dandy-fever" to signify a disease called "dengue." The third meaning of the word, dating from 1685, tells us that "dandy" was an Anglo-Indian name for the boatmen of the Ganges. The historical broadcast of quite alien associations, to use Pater's way of describing such semantic reverberation, reveals a colonial repressed and its return on each side of the word's otherwise aristocratic connotation. The term "dandy" is, as it were, perpetually shadowed by its opposite, whether it means the British soldier and the American, the imperialist and the boatman, or a native plague and some Anglified distance from it.

How did this dubious shell of an aristocratic style become so durable? Here we must turn our attention across the Channel, to France. A belated Romanticism and a prescient aestheticism, dandyism—indeed, French Romanticism itself—is the major entr'acte between High British Romanticism and Pater. Barbey d'Aurevilly's biography of Brummell in 1845 was the "bridge," as Moers puts it, between English and French dandyism (1960, 257), and Barbey's "originality," she writes, "is to make dandyism available as an intellectual pose" (1960, 263). Barbey's serious Catholicism later in his career even presages rumors, for example, about Pater's growing interest in religion late in his own career, although in Pater's case the interest was sensory rather than theological. But while dandyism in France was at first allied, as it had been in England, with aristocratic styles seeking to reestablish some credibility after the revolution of 1830, it also became allied with the rather different project of an emergent bohemian Paris. The birth of a self-conscious bohemian Paris in 1830 combined dandyism and bohemia—what Jerrold Seigel calls "the Bohemian-dandy symbiosis" in *Bohemian Paris* (1986, 105)—and produced the beginnings of the search for a public style that suited its ambitions. Despite class and political differences, "bohemia" is in retrospect probably the best umbrella term, short of the more exacting term "aestheticism," to account for the variety of notions of what dandyism is and what it represents. Many youngsters went to Paris after 1830, setting a sturdy pattern that still exists today in Paris and in other cityscapes from New York to Seattle.

In "The Painter of Modern Life" (1859–60), Baudelaire, following in the tradition of Barbey's Brummell, collapses the difference between dandyism as a style of the idle rich and dandyism as a quite different "aristocratic superiority of mind" (1859–60, 27). He then gives us an uncannily Paterian definition of the dandy as an intellectual type: "The burning need to create for oneself a personal originality" (1859–60, 27), "a kind of cult of the self" (27), "a kind of religion" (28). All dandies, whatever their official politics, possess the same characteristic quality of "opposition and revolt" (28). One is reminded of Marlon Brando's reply to the question "What are you kids against?" in Laslo Benedek's *The Wild One* (1954): "What," he asks, "have you got?" The dandy's is "a latent fire," and, at least before Pater, the dandy "chooses," in a double retrospective jest, "not to burst into flame" (29).

Thus "Anglomania" in bohemian Paris after 1830, says Moers, "made the dandy and the romantic one and the same" (1960, 121). It should, however, also be remembered, she says, that the English High Romantics and the original world of the English dandy were themselves at odds from the point of view of social class (1960, 51), even though, by the second half of the nineteenth century, late Romantic aestheticism and dandyism are nonetheless of a piece, as the example of Wilde makes perfectly clear. The "dandy," writes Richard Pine in his revisionary account of Moers's history, and "the aesthete" are "synonymous" (1988, 31). Likewise, Seigel's distinction in *Bohemian Paris* between the political dandyism of Baudelaire and the aristocractic dandyism of Gautier is really a descriptive rather than an epistemological one. Gautier's absolute aestheticism in the notorious preface to *Mademoiselle de Maupin* (1834, 1835) eschews all politics and social concern, particularly a belief in human "perfectibility" (xxvii–xxviii), as Gautier puts it, while Baudelaire's aestheticism, by contrast, sent him to the barricades in the Revolution of 1848 (the difference in England between Disraeli the Tory at midcentury and the dandyism of the Decadence at its close is a reverse version of this same descriptive split). Seigel also notes this very difference within Baudelaire himself—the difference between a "self-contained dandyism" (1986, 124) on the one hand and "the Bohemian need to live for the multiplication of sensation" (124) on the other. Baudelaire's desire for a "multiplication of sensation," argues Seigel, was his "real heroism" (124) and his route to a radical politics, an opening out onto the world and toward a pleasure in the "vagabond life" (109) and a fondness for the "crowd" (114). His "self-contained dandyism"—even the dandyism of the crowd-loving *flâneur*—was a more private affair.

Walter Benjamin, however, draws a more intimate relation between these two impulses in "On Some Motifs in Baudelaire" (1939), suggesting an entirely aesthetic motivation to be behind them both. In "Paris, Capital of the Nineteenth Century" (1955), Benjamin remarks that the flâneur—Seigel's presumably political creature—actually presents an "uncertainty" of "political function" (1955, 156). Seigel's two Baudelaires ultimately derive from the same desire for stimulation: the multiplied sensation that leads to a delight in the crowd and the "self-contained dandyism" that leads to a recoiling from the world are really the poles of a single aestheticist structure. Nor are they absolute poles, but poles in a crossing over—a structure of interdependence—that puts the boundaries between self and world into place. A brief reading of Baudelaire as poet will help to illuminate it.

In "La Vie antérieure" (1855), a sonnet included in *Les Fleurs du mal* (1857), interiority is, ironically, a product of anteriority or pastness—of that which comes before. Despite the transcendentalizing impulses normally assigned to the poem (including the customary translation of the title as "Former Life"), it actually shows how one's inwardness, purportedly the realm of the personally authentic, is actually a function of precursor languages that allow for—that help to make—the place of authentic, reflective selfhood to begin with. Selfhood, the "self-contained," is, ironically, a function of the historical and the social. Indeed, to have to "create an originality," as Baudelaire says in his essay, means that it is not simply there on its own. The interior life requires an anterior life that is also, by definition, exterior to the self, even if it is what structures the self. The poem has a precursor poem behind it, too. "La Vie antérieure" sounds like Keats's "On First Looking into Chapman's Homer" (1816). Compare the openings of the two poems, which are both sonnets and which are measured in very similar ways. "Much have I travell'd in the realms of gold, / And many goodly states and kingdoms seen," says Keats (1–2); "J'ai longtemps habité," answers Baudelaire, "sous de vastes portiques / Que les soleils marins teignaient de mille feux" (1–2). Nor is there a shared Petrarchan source, since neither sonnet celebrates an object, only a subject, which is, paradoxically, each poem's object. The anterior life for Baudelaire here is Keats's poem, much as the anterior life for Keats is Chapman's translation of Homer. The anterior for Keats and Baudelaire alike is the history of poetic usage and mythology that precedes them both.

With some irony, each poem also equates an animated interior landscape with the landscape of the New World. In the process, Keats's sonnet exchanges Homer with Cortez the explorer (11, in a famous error—it should be Balboa), replacing the ancient father with the American newcomer. More directly, Baudelaire identifies landscapes of interior sensation with landscapes of empire (12), the latter historically Christian as well as synecdoches for France's own colonial conquests. Like Keats, too, Baudelaire's vision of the interior is also, paradoxically, one that identifies refreshment (12) with dolor and languor (14), the price, presumably, of his relative belatedness. Keats himself overcomes just this characteristic propensity of his own imagination in the Chapman sonnet, although by teasing it out in this context Baudelaire also manages to turn Keats's own momentarily resolved belatedness back into a difficulty that he negotiates with seemingly greater awareness than does the Englishman. Refreshment, originality, authenticity based upon anteriority—these are painfully purchased by the necessity of past representations that, with deadly irony, secure a presumably interior life for the poet in his own transient present. For Keats and Baudelaire alike, selfhood is itself procured by crossing over. To have an inside requires an outside from which an inside can be different, much as the self's defining sense of immediacy requires the self to have, or at least to imagine, an anteriority, a formerness, a history, a past—a series of boundaries—against or upon which its sense of the present can prop itself. Precursor languages and mythological systems are the anteriority that give personal interiority both a structure and a content. Here the interdependence of the "self-contained" and "multiplied sensation" is very clear indeed.

In the larger history of the dandy, another point is also deliciously clear. French Romanticism's reinvention of the dandy eventually makes its way back to England and finds its intellectual organization in Pater (Pine 1988, 65 ff.). Much as Emerson prefigures Western expansion and gives its ideology a basis or a ground, so Pater formalizes a social movement coming up under and before him and for which he, the presumably great solitary, comes to speak. Hence Pater's own interiority, too, is a function of the kind of aesthetic mechanism described by Keats and Baudelaire alike, a relation to something outside himself. Like his attachment to lemon-kid gloves, Pater's reading in French Romantic fiction and poetry garnished his own Romantic sensibility (see Inman 1981, 1990) and heightens the irony with which the structure of Paterian inwardness is furnished a motivation beyond the anxiety of Ruskin's influence in the mythologies of bohemian Paris.

While Pater's *Studies in the History of the Renaissance,* including the notorious "Conclusion" that was suppressed in the book's second edition, stirred an enormous public storm upon its publication in 1873 (one is reminded of the reception of *Les Fleurs du mal* in Paris in 1857), the renovation of the dandy as a serious aesthetic figure was by now commonplace enough in England. Browning, the Pre-Raphaelites, even Dickens all cut swashing figures as variously striking as their work. Indeed, the model of Byron had given the dandy an intellectual authority from the beginning. Sarah Blake even suggests that it is through the Brontës that Byronism passes directly to Pater, who, like Emerson, stabilizes a mythology by affording it its highest expression. Even though his own affinities are more with Wordsworth and Coleridge than with Shelley, for whom Emerson is an especially boon companion, Pater shares with Emerson a Shelleyan—and a Byronic—fascination with the dynamics of the boundaries that shape subjects and objects alike, a fascination that structures his career early and late. Like Turner's charting of the American West as "the interior" (1893, 20), or like Poe's notion of the imagination as, in Jack Sullivan's words, "an alternate frontier" (1994, 91), Pater secures his stabilities by virtue of crossing over, sometimes in the form of the temporal reversals practiced by Poe's French translator, Baudelaire. In *Marius the Epicurean* (1885), for example, the freshness of Christianity becomes available to the novel's hero by virtue of the narrative protocols of classical learning, the very protocols that Christianity presumably supersedes, much as, in a chiasmus, the belated truth of Christianity retroactively enlightens classicism by rendering it, belatedly, a mode of Christian narrative. This is certainly not to regard "reality as simulation" (Felski 1991, 1097), as one scholar of dandyism puts it, since such a view returns us to the dualism between fact and fiction that is overcome both in

Baudelaire and in Pater himself. Boundaries, like those of the New World, are put into place by the transgression of the very proper-ness—of the *propre,* of that which is one's own—that boundaries supposedly represent.

What, then, is the technology of the dandyism or aestheticism that Pater formalizes? One of the great ironies of the "Conclusion" is that Pater's attempt to give a different vision of the world from within and from without collapses into a single vision, suggesting, as does Emerson, that there is neither inside nor outside as such. Like Shelley and Emerson both, Pater is interested in how the world happens. What is, asks Pater, even "physical life"?

> a perpetual motion [he answers] . . . the passage of the blood, the wasting and repairing of the lenses of the eye, the modification of the tissues of the brain by every ray of light and sound. . . . Like the elements of which we are composed, the action of these forces ex-tends beyond us; it rusts iron and ripens corn. Far out on every side of us those elements are broadcast, driven by many forces; and birth and gesture and death and the springing of violets from the grave are but a few out of ten thousand resultant combinations. That clear, per-petual outline of face and limb is but an image of ours, under which we group them—a design in a web, the actual threads of which pass out beyond it. (1873, 59)

Things become entirely clear in the next paragraph:

> When reflexion begins to act upon those objects they are dissipated under its influence; the cohesive force seems suspended like a trick of magic; each object is loosed into a group of impressions—colour, odour, texture—in the mind of the observer. (59)

Although such a vision leads Pater to lament its consequences be-cause it seems to result in the individual's isolation—the distress-ingly "narrow chamber of the individual mind," "each mind keep-ing as a solitary prisoner its own dream of a world" (59–60)—any phenomenological distinction between self and world has already been put in question despite the emotional inevitabilities involved. Indeed, the paragraph announcing Pater's famous solipsism ends with the reverberant phrase that undoes it, "that strange, perpetual weaving and unweaving of ourselves" (60). Solipsism depends upon its counterpart in vacancy, weaving upon unweaving, form upon formlessness.

This loosening of the boundaries that put the universe of things in place, this perpetual weaving and unweaving of the frontiers that demarcate subjects and objects alike—this is Pater's psychedelic sublime, a paradoxical experience of ecstasy that, by definition, undoes experience itself by undoing the subjectivity that experiences it. The psychedelic is the play of boundaries that organizes the clear in relation to the chaos against which it emerges. Although the Greek noun *delos* means the clear or visible, its Latin permutations include the verb *delilare,* the root of delirium, meaning to deviate from a straight line. Thus the psychedelic, even etymologically, reflexively redoubles the shifting status of boundaries that aestheticism thematizes. The play of the clear in relation to chaos is a paradigm for the way opposites define one another in Pater's epistemology. The psychedelic puts the subject, him or herself, at perpetual risk as the price of his or her own experience (for the reduced twentieth-century version, see Leary 1964). Even gender assignments fluctuate under the psychedelic sublime, as Jessica R. Feldman shows in *Gender on the Divide* (1993), a fluctuation apparent, as she argues, from bohemian Paris to Willa Cather and, we should add, to Bloomsbury. This weaving and unweaving of the frontiers that zone subjects and objects alike is also Pater's profound secularization of Shelley's—and Emerson's—vision of a world. Subjects and objects are reciprocal functions one of the other in what is really an implicit theory of ideology that Wilde will go on to make explicit. Like Shelley and like Emerson, but in an even franker way, Pater's real subject is the making and unmaking of boundaries as such.

Pater's epistemology of the poet is very like Emerson's and Shelley's, too. Why is Leonardo, for example, important? Because, as the well-known passage on the Mona Lisa shows, his work is a sufficient receptacle and organizer of otherwise unconnected roads of discursive sway to connect and orchestrate them influentially (1873, 46–47). Indeed, the very notion of genius, mastership, or canonical status in "The School of Giorgione" is the same, too, although its terms have been novelized into the drama of an artist's workshop. If a student perfectly imitates the master's style in the execution or completion of a painting, whose name properly belongs to it? Form as such is always social, whether the form in question is subject or object. Given the psychedelic sublime, form itself is a mode of repression, a reduction, a choice in the midst of the weaving and un-weaving that is *la vraie vérité*. "Our failure," says a staunch Pater in the "Conclusion," "is to form habits" (1873, 60). The unitariness that meaning and action alike require as categories becomes especially offensive in this light. The psychedelic or semiotic sublime is a quantitative sublime, the rush that comes from disrupting normative bonds of reference and association in favor of the new and potentially endless associations to be had from the collision, reverberation, and recombination of old ones.

This indictment of the social by the psychedelic has a surprising implication, even though a familiar structural reason lies behind it. The social is, as it turns out, the only force that provides structure in an otherwise formless world. What coherence there is to life is the result of the organizing power of "habits," to use Pater's word, a "failure," as he calls it, from the point of view of the sublime, but an inevitability from the point of view of necessity. No wonder the psychedelic bohemia of the 1960s was torn between a personal and a political agenda—between a revolutionary politics on the one hand and a deep inwardness on the other. Such a conflict recalls the same conflict in the Parisian bohemia of Baudelaire's dandy and finds a counterpart in Pater's own double vision. This is, however, no conflict at all, but a sober interdependence. Psychedelic vision gives us, to use Pater's Heraclitean formulation, all things in flux. But this flux also reveals how sadly precious the world of social order is, since it is our only bulwark against absolute chaos. In this sense, the psychedelic bohemia of the 1960s was also a clear chapter in the larger history of the dandy, since it showed how each pole in a presumable conflict between self and society was bound to the other. Even the self is a social fiction, and even society is an inevitable invention. This is the surpassing crossing over of the dandy's bohemia. The title of R. D. Laing's popular 1960s text *The Politics of Experience* (1967) well exemplifies this loop, suggesting as it does that experience—the world of the individual—has a social dimension, just as the social—the collective world—can be known only by means of personal experience.

Pater's doubleness, then, recapitulates the split within dandyism, a split whose rhythm or balance between worldiness and withdrawal has no better turn-of-the-century representative than the dandy detective, Sherlock Holmes. Arthur Conan Doyle's bohemian hero well exemplifies the crossing structure of the dandy from Baudelaire and Gautier to Pater, Wilde, Aubrey Beardsley, and Max Beerbohm, and serves as a useful summary of its inevitabilities. The crafty precisions of Jeremy Brett's television Holmes helpfully rediscovers the Wildean Holmes's dandy style and stance in a revisionary reading of Basil Rathbone's sedate Hollywood Holmes, making the systematic doubleness of Conan Doyle's creation very plain indeed. The aesthetic or bohemian atmosphere of Baker Street is itself, of course, manifest. Watson remarks upon Holmes's "natural Bohemianism of disposition" at the start of "The Musgrave Ritual" (1894, 386) and upon Holmes's "Bohemian soul" at the start of "A Scandal in Bohemia" (1892a, 161). Watson even describes the rhythm of Holmes's daily life in a rhetorical loop: "He alternated," says Watson, "between cocaine and ambition, the drowsiness of the drug and the fierce energy of his own nature" (1892a, 161).

This crossing is a microcosm of the loop that as a rule structures both Holmes himself and his relation to Watson. Their partnership is a crossing of the bizarre and the responsible, the wild and the sober. Holmes the dandy's self-containment is regularly put in the service of solving crime for the good of society, while Watson's medical sociality is regularly put in the service of his self-contained relation to Holmes. Indeed, Holmes the aesthete paradoxically prefers a literary realism that is scientific when he regularly criticizes Watson's lurid prose style, while Watson the medical man practices a prose style that is, as Holmes correctly points out, often very Romantic indeed. Of course, Holmes is hardly dispassionate despite his scientific preferences, waxing especially eloquent when he objects to Watson's belief in the seeming peace and beauty of the countryside in "The Copper Beeches" (1892b):

> The reason is very obvious. The pressure of public opinion can do in the town what the law cannot accomplish. There is no lane so vile that the scream of a tortured child, or the thud of a drunkard's blow, does not beget sympathy and indignation among the neighbours, and then the whole machinery of justice is never so close that a word of complaint can set it going, and there is but a step between the crime and the dock. But look at these lonely houses, each in its own fields, filled for the most part with poor ignorant folk who know little of the law. Think of the deeds of hellish cruelty, the hidden wickedness which may go on, year in, year out, in such places, and none the wiser. (1892b, 323)

Here Holmes stuns his companion with a bristling reversal of the customary relation between country and city. For Holmes, the cruel city is lawful, while the gentle country is lawless. Nature is not only very lonely and unreliable; it is "'hellish.'" The city, by contrast, is full of "'sympathy.'" Like Wilde—and like Wilde's cowboy confreres—Holmes "wishes," to use Wilde's words in "The Decay of Lying," "to teach Nature her proper place" (1891, 291).

In keeping with Holmes's aestheticism, Conan Doyle indulges in an outright play on the term "Bohemia" that follows it back to its roots and that shows how its origins as a trope actually double or dramatize what it signifies. Not for nothing does Watson remark upon Holmes's "Bohemian soul" at the start of "A Scandal in Bohemia." The story sets up an ironic reverberation between the two senses of the word, the "Bohemia" of the aesthete and the "Bohemia" of Holmes's client in the story, the king of Bohemia. Aesthetic bohemia takes its name from the old belief that the wandering, nomadic gypsies originated in the kingdom of Bohemia, or what today we call the Czech Republic. Holmes's client is, by contrast, hardly a wanderer. As the king of Bohemia, he is the most landed, the most grounded of all Bohemians; he presides over the same Bohemia through which gypsy Bohemians merely pass. Thus the proper sense of the word collides with its second, wandering sense; aesthetic bohemia undoes the home of habit, or usage, of ruling, grounded Bohemia, including the capital letter that designates the proper(ty)—the proper name—it eschews. On home ground, the trope "Bohemia" reflexively enacts its own difference from itself. Bohemian king and bohemian nomad, ground and psychedelic "loosening," to use Pater's word—this is the crossing play that, like gypsies crossing Bohemia, defines the aesthetic against the proper and the proper against the aesthetic, the play that defines each "Bohemia" as a difference from the other.

Holmes's assault upon nature also helps us to answer a larger question. What do cowboy and dandy share? Why was Wilde as comfortable with the cowboys in Colorado as they appeared to be with him? What vision do they hold in common? Their relation, as it turns out, is a crossing one, too, a loop that connects them while at the same time distinguishing them one from the other. If the aesthete or dandy sees nature as empty and culture as full, the cowboy sees nature as full and culture as empty. The cowboy's richly savage nature is a vital presence, while the dandy's pale nature is all absence. The cowboy's nature is a promised land; the dandy's is, as Holmes puts it, "'hellish.'" Nature's blankness or lawlessness allows the cowboy to fill it with a mythological significance derived from culture, repressing and dismissing culture in the process in order to gain a higher sense of nature. Nature's blankness allows the dandy, by contrast, to value culture's fullness by virtue of an ironic contrast, too, gaining an even higher sense of culture in the process. Between them a heightened sense of nature and culture alike becomes available, and, perhaps even more, a heightened and ironic sense of the fluctuating boundaries, the endless crossings back and forth, that put each end of the loop into place.

5

"I SECOND THAT EMOTION"

As rhythm and blues develops into the premier mode of blues tradition in the late Fifties, Sixties, and Seventies, the dominant singers of each of these eras refine our paradigm with extraordinary precision. Otis Redding's rapacious voice, for example, explores the endless postures appropriate to the band driving it from behind, amazing us with the multiplicity of stances and tonalities through which it can flash, each of which has a stable tie to the sharp horns and deep rhythm section of Booker T. Jones's Stax studio ensemble. Voice, horns, and rhythm section among them stage any series of dialogues or dialectics instead of fortifying a hierarchic relation between band and voice alone. The shouts remind us that this is indeed merely a person singing, even though their sheer percussiveness also takes away the very difference between voice and instruments that the shouting seems to advance. Like Armstrong, Redding crosses a dirty tone with legato phrasing, but, unlike Armstrong, he also needs the unabashed screams to reinvent Armstrong's crossing from country to city, recovering the field holler that Armstrong himself absorbs. Redding crosses back again to the country from the city, reimagining blues tradition by virtue of the preacherly stance from which his vocal inflections also derive. He uses gospel to revise Armstrong, but he also uses Armstrong to revise gospel. Here Redding makes the structure of mature, achieved r & b or soul music altogether clear: the crossing of blues and gospel, like the crossing of blues with country, is another kind of trick played at or by the crossroads. Like the belatedness of raw electric blues after Charlie Christian, gospel is a mode of seemingly pure, fresh enthusiasm that is actually historically belated, too—the style as we know it begins only with Thomas Dorsey in the 1920s. It also provides a new aesthetic effect with which to counter or resist what is by now the evolved, refined sound of jazz itself. The ironic aesthetic sense of hearing and playing something older, more primal, more original than jazz proper is, like that of urban blues, the new gospel's uncanny signature as it develops from gospel to soul itself.

Aretha Franklin dramatizes our paradigm in readily newer rhythm and blue terms, too. The great Muscle Shoals rhythm section with which she worked at Atlantic Records after leaving Columbia in 1966 features the lyrical drummer Roger Hawkins behind her rhythmic voice, a contrast that switches the role assignments customary to voice and instrument while, of course, also preserving them thanks to Hawkins's remarkable groove and Franklin's own soaring lyricism. The purity of Franklin's gospel phrasing in contrast—and complement—to the graininess of the rhythm section is an equally efficient picture of crossing over and pressures its own success as a function of it. Franklin's lofty voice and the downfunk of the band are clearly different, although the voice's purity is also proof that it, too, is an instrument even more refined than those behind it. Franklin's ductile relation to the Muscle Shoals rhythm section has any number of analogs in the way rhythm and blues singing at large tends to break down oppositions as a function of exercising them.

The line of influence that moves from Jackie Wilson (1934–1984) to Smokey Robinson (b. 1940) and Al Green (b. 1946) is an especially clear one that rearticulates the structural regularities familiar to us within a rhythm and blues context. Here natural and falsetto voice registers take on the roles of country and city. As precursor to Robinson and Green alike (and, together with Sam Cooke, to Marvin Gaye, who died by his father's hand in 1984), Wilson develops a paradigmatic r & b vocal style based on a play between natural and falsetto that has roots in the earliest sources of blues tradition, and whose own direct precursor sound is doowop, blues tradition's reinvention of barbershop quartet. Falsetto is one of two styles of Delta blues late in the nineteenth century, one "rough," one "falsetto" (Morgan and Barlow 1992, 29), and a disposition of voice recognizable in African sources well beforehand (Charters 1981, 119).

Wilson begins as a doowopper, replacing Clyde McPhatter as the lead singer for the doowop Dominoes in 1953 before launching out on his own in 1956. He transforms doowop into a single vocal style by transistorizing the roles assigned to each voice separately into the design of a single singer's voice. It is ultimately a call-and-response arrangement, of course, a contraction of the quartet into a dialogue, and polished by doowop's characteristic urbanity, although the dialogue is now the dialogue of the voice with itself. It is the inner version, as it were, of call-and-response, and its presumably psychological effects rest on the difference between falsetto and natural registers alone. Wilson invents, out of the inevitability of the device from doowop tradition in particular and blues usage at large, a vocal style that exploits the splitting of the voice in two, making its self-reflection its major characteristic.

Falsetto has to do not so much with gender—those associations are secondary—as with a means to the heightened instrumentalization of voice. Falsetto is not a sign of degeneresence or of alienation either but of an increase and expansion of the powers of the voice musically. Little Richard's leaps into falsetto, however biographically they may be construed, are leaps into a higher musical possibility, not a deeper personal one. Falsetto countervails the natural, foils the thick depth of the male register. False and natural display themselves one against the other, making the contrast between direct and contrived, nature and culture, very plain indeed, but also showing how entirely interdependent they are. Wilson's r & b mode is the art that feeds off these contrasts. It is what Smokey Robinson overcomes in Wilson by being seemingly artificial, postmodern, postsexual. It is also what Al Green retrieves and hyperbolizes in Wilson to gain his own signature style, which is, like Wilson's own, a dialogue of the voice with its own possibilities, particularly in relation to precedent. Let us consider Wilson first before turning to his acolytes.

BY BRINGING TOGETHER the dynamics of doowop into the artifice of a single voice, Wilson renders the meaning of single or given voice problematic. His phrasing as a rule plays natural and falsetto registers off against each other in sequence. While at times both are simultaneously at work in a cool, modulated grain, his achieved ease is more typically the equipoise of two registers in endless conversation. When Wilson jumps on "you," for example, on "Lonely Teardrops" (1958), it is to extend the range of the instrument of his voice beyond what is natural to it, as the saying goes, and, by force of musical will, to construct an additional register and a half beyond voice's natural possibilities. On "Reet Petite" (1957)—future Motown mogul Berry Gordy's first published song and Wilson's first hit—the crossing between natural and falsetto ranges is what the song is all about. As astonishing as Wilson's natural voice is, his falsetto voice is even more stunning, a difference or crossing that calls overriding attention to itself and to the art of contrasts that it represents. Wilson's technical prowess alone is remarkable, but its chief feature—a tenor singer's command of falsetto registers—is what makes him an exception to the potential banalities of the customary tradition of tenor singing alone. (Of course, as a straight Irish tenor in operatic mode, Wilson is also superb, with his virtuosic recording of "Danny Boy" [1965a] the best evidence of it.) "Reet Petite" is really a swinging blues, with horns out of the swing era. Wilson's articulation of "so fine" in the second chorus is an *hommage,* however brief, to bop phrasing. Nevertheless, the dialogue between and among vocal registers persists throughout and grounds the song, however peripatetically—"all right" is moaned out Delta style twice in the last verse, for example, right next to the dandified phrasing of "got what it takes."

If "Reet Petite" emphasizes the falsetto Wilson, "I'll Be Satisfied" (1959b) emphasizes the natural Wilson, who jumps into falsetto only during the tune's last chorus. When he sings "tell me" or "sleep in my lonely bed" on a ballad like "Please Tell Me Why" (1961a), he splits his voice regularly between the two. On a song like "No Pity" (1965b), by contrast, both stances are displayed in the first verse, but by the chorus, Wilson's voice actually resolves the contradictory trends and registers it has just shown into one hard if torn force. Then, after remaining surprisingly uniform until the story line starts again in the next verse with "You go walking down Broadway," it cracks back into doubleness or self-division. At tune's end, a swing band bed subtends the dialogue of Wilson's voice with itself, easing the differences as they mate over jazz while simultaneously maintaining their distinctness more starkly than ever. The component impulses of Wilson's voice do not, of course, interfere with one another; they need each other. On "You Don't Know What It Means" (1961b), "means" is the semantic site chosen for displaying the qualities in the fissured rock of Wilson's sound. On "That's Why" (1959a), you hear two registers in one very clearly; on a ballad like "A Woman, a Lover, a Friend" (1960), Wilson jumps registers with peculiar force, perhaps in resistance to the sodden production.

Of Wilson's greatest hits, "Baby Workout" (1963) is the greatest. It is, arguably, the most pivotal and exemplary rock and roll song ever. At once a swing and a rhythm and blues or soul tune—Wilson's gospel phrasing over a swing bottom makes it definitive rock and roll—it is a model of crossing over at every level of its construction. It orchestrates any series of familiar oppositions—natural and falsetto, voice and instrument, country and city, blues and gospel, secular and sacred—while also undoing the borders that keep them in place. Even the lyrics redouble our paradigm in a clear way: the song actually reflects on the uncertainty of boundaries. "Round and around and around and around we go," sings Wilson; "where we stop nobody knows." Where is the line between swing and rhythm and blues, jazz and rock and roll? Between city and country, subject and object, self and world? Like Emerson, Pater, Woolf, and Cather—and, of course, like Muddy Waters and Chuck Berry—Wilson finally meditates on form as such.

SMOKEY ROBINSON AND THE MATADORS (the Miracles' original name) auditioned for Jackie Wilson's manager in 1957, when Robinson also met Berry Gordy (see Gordy 1994, 84 ff.). The power and the persuasiveness of internal evidence alone, however, is enough to suggest that Robinson's singing is in many ways the result of a revisionary relation to Wilson from the start ("Got a Job" [1957], for example, a local Detroit hit, is a Wilsonesque doowop song). Robinson's durably recognizable originality—he is probably the most imitated voice in the later history of rhythm and blues—depends in large part upon a strong misreading, as the saying goes, of the enabling but burdensome precursor. While Sarah Vaughan is, by his own testimony, his manifest and conscious influence (1989, 49), underneath it is Wilson. If Wilson exploits the poles of doowop exchange, then Robinson resolves them into the achieved singularity of an uninterruptedly falsetto style, even though he will often let us in on their connectedness by sliding back and forth on the shifting boundary between them. Let us glance at some of his major hits to see how his relation to Wilson functions.

"I Second That Emotion" (1967), a tune Robinson cowrote with Al Cleveland (with whom he cowrote seven of the Miracles' next eight hits), is a model for his work as a whole. The song interrogates its own melody as the melody's actual narrative line—undoing itself, undercutting itself with each phrase, unbuilding itself as the ironic mode of its building. The lyrics explain why the song is constructed this way, rhyming "emotion" and even "devotion" with the unlikely "notion" in order to make a startling claim that reverses our customary sense of the relation of feeling to form. Emotion emerges out of personality's tie to vernacular forms, the latter always organizing the bonds between and among individuals. By crossing excruciatingly beautiful singing with greeting-card idioms, Robinson shows how each one lends the other credence and irony alike. The title of the song is an announcement writ large of the derived nature of feeling itself (no wonder it's a pun on quorum rules), of the reductions to which the natural is subject even to be natural (Robinson's indebtedness to Wilson is the reflexive version of the process). The melody line's phantom allusiveness adds to the effect as it downsteps a scale back into the verse. A jazz residue is palpable in the production as well, an essentially Memphis arrangement garnished with bop harmonics selectively applied to parts and melodies alike (see George 1985, 177). Indeed, the genius of Gordy's studio sound is that it produces a depth of field, giving it an archaeological rather than a cinematic impressiveness, perhaps because it is structured downward from its surface rather than across it. On faster Motown tunes such as Martha and the Vandellas' "Heat Wave" (1963), Gordy's archaeology includes not only bop harmonics but also a Chicago blues shuffle beat, two styles that are presumably at odds but that Gordy makes continuous. Robinson himself thought of Motown, he says, as "a university" (1989, 212).

How does Robinson deal with the Wilson influence? Why do we recognize "I Second That Emotion" as the Robinson that we know and love? Because, like "Ooo Baby Baby" (1965a), it collapses Wilson's double-register singing into a largely single falsetto style even more doowoppy than Wilson's own. An artificial accomplishment that fights fire with fire, Robinson rewrites the past by resolving

Wilson's own doubleness. Even though the absolute falsetto is not always Robinson's style, it is the voice we most remember, and the result of the most radical of his responses to the Wilson precedent. Nor is Robinson's falsetto evenness gendered or even personal. Libido has been sublimated into work, poured into the music; little is left over to distinguish a biography behind the voice. Much as rock and roll as a rule undoes categories of race, so Robinson's singing, like Wilson's, undoes sexual characteristics in voice as part of an aesthetic imperative. The voice's only identity is musical. It is testimony to a triumph within a tradition as well as a surpassing example of how such triumph is managed: by preserving the past while simultaneously revising it.

Like the reflexive address to the medium on "Going to a Go Go" (1965c), "The Tracks of My Tears" (1965b) tells us why there are tears—because tradition renders the latecomer secondary in life and art alike. Subject and object are both produced within its whirlpool of convention and exchange. "She's just a substitute," drawls Robinson, lamenting the fact that the beloved is, like the singer who loves, a perpetual surrogate for "the permanent one" that can never be found. Any satisfaction or achievement lacks the ground it presumably bestows. Its terms are derived, not original. "Tracks of My Tears" also gives us a surpassing instance of Robinson's resolution of Wilson's influence—turning the split in Wilson's voice into a single vocal strategy that retrieves the doowopper in Wilson himself, especially the falsetto doowopper. Is "tears" a pun, as writing if not as sung speech? After all, Robinson "tears" through the clear difference in Wilson between the two registers, creating a kind of ragged space of his own between what in Wilson are separate and distinct realms.

TO SITUATE AL GREEN within the sphere of Wilson's influence is simple enough biographically. His father threw him out of the family gospel band—and out of the house—when he caught him listening to a Jackie Wilson record. What did the young Green make of Wilson? Or, rather, what did Wilson make of the young Green? Robert Christgau has described Al Green as "self-alienated" (1992, 510), a term borrowed from Hardy's *The Mayor of Casterbridge* (1886, 380) and one that well describes both Green's ironic achievement and how he got there musically. His "self-alienation" is the effect of an extraordinarily self-conscious and strategic singing style, a throwback to Wilson's dialogue of the soul with itself. Like Robinson, he returns to Wilson, but he handles him differently. If Robinson resolves Wilson's split or double voice into a single falsetto style, then Green splits it back open again, retrieving precisely the strategy that Robinson changes: the distinctness of the two registers, the overt self-conversation. As a rule, the sequencing of Green's phrasing narrates it as a newly witting dialogue between natural and falsetto registers that becomes his own vocal signature. Even when he combines natural and falsetto in a grainy doubleness, he is responding to the past. His voice is a compact crushing—a kind of junk or scrap metaling—of influences, a strength forged out of the shards of prior vocal usages. In normal register he reaches down inside the sound, belly out, although what bottom there may be keeps turning to texture, to the shifting grounds of influence upon which any artist works. The very category of voice—of voice as the expression of a single self—is upset by Green's vocal praxis, which disperses among the texts that determine it the fugitive unity that his skill alone is capable of achieving as the illusion unified voice is. Crossing is even the customary structural device of the melody hooks on his most characteristic tunes.

Let's Stay Together (1972) and its title tune, released as a single in 1971, remain Green's most characteristic—and still his best—achievement, especially in light of his turn to the religious in the years since 1980. Lou Christie's old lyric "Two Faces Have I" (1963) well describes Green's characteristic strategy here: the overt dialogue of natural and falsetto registers that retrieves Wilson, and the compaction of registers that represses him. On "So You're Leaving," it takes Green two falsetto fillips on the first verse before his voice unwinds, unpacks, relaxes, and becomes itself, as it were, as though he must survey the ground before letting the customary "self-alienated" conversation begin. Despite the counterpoint of the back-up singers and the Memphis Horns, the conversation is one not with the band but with the self, whatever that entity has now become. On "Old Time Lovin'," Green moves through both low crankiness and a high-register shout before he settles down, especially in his improvisatory use of the word "time" to stage the conversation one expects from him. "I've Never Found a Girl Like You" has the air of a singer so sure of himself that you wonder how all the textures can be combined with such control. That's what the singer goes on to ask, too. "She's everything," he sings in falsetto; "she's every poor boy's dream," he sings in natural register. During the vamp at tune's end, the conversation between natural and falsetto takes over entirely even before the fade begins.

A Bee Gees tune, the ballad "How Can You Mend a Broken Heart?" well equals "Let's Stay Together" in depth and power. Verse and chorus between them play out the dialogue of the voice with itself. "I can still feel the breeze," sings a Coleridgean Green as he negotiates the winds of influence that blast through his various voices. That's why his "heart" is "broken." "No one told us," says a Bloomian Green, "about the sorrows"—the sorrows of influence. "It Ain't No Fun" is, at first, the most conventional Memphis tune on the album, featuring stomping guitar and pumping bass. But the ensemble solidity is in sharp contrast to the singing, which moves in and out of self-synthesis in tone and phrasing alike, and so narrates the impossible struggle to be one that is characteristic of this "self-alienated" singer's project as a whole.

The title of "Let's Stay Together" is, of course, a reflexive one; the song addresses itself. Here all options are available to Green's voice. As he delivers the end of the tune's chorus—"it's all right with me"—he splits the "me" between natural and falsetto, sliding down from one to the other. It is no surprise that the word "me" is the semantic site of the song's principal vocal slipping and sliding, since the sliding undoes the very category of unified voice to which "me" customarily refers. Green's address to a beloved—"Let's stay together"—is also an ironic and summary commentary upon his own self-alienation. It is an impossible appeal to tradition to help him mend a heart that tradition itself has given him.

6

the COWBOY, the DANDY, and WILLA CATHER

Everyone knows that literary modernism is related to blues tradition, but no one knows just how. The common preoccupation with boundaries, however, gives us the clue we need as we cross over from the nineteenth to the twentieth century in our literary travels. Dominant culture's customary estimation of the kinship between jazz and modern literature is well represented by the primitivism that both presumably share, a primitivism whose language and assumptions D. H. Lawrence, for example, makes abundantly clear in his reading of Freud in 1921. However unintentionally, Lawrence's metaphor of "the darkness" (1921, 5) into which Freud the explorer descends links modern imagination with expansionism and colonialism, and links them both, as Lawrence's American disciple Norman Mailer will go on to show in *The White Negro* (1957) and *An American Dream* (1965), to a negotiation with the savage energy assigned to blackness as though it were the eruption of pure natural force. Like nature in blues tradition, however, nature in modernism is more often the occasion for a meditation on form than the expression of a primitive state paradoxically—and problematically—represented by black culture and its achievements.

Willa Cather's fiction has an exemplary role in American literary modernism because it breaks down the same mystifications about nature that blues tradition does. Cather's novels dramatize in thematic as well as rhetorical ways the the loops or crossings that we have seen at work in electric blues and rhythm and blues, and recapitulate the selfsame structures that produce in earlier Romantic tradition the boundaries that install as inevitable foils or counterparts the illusions of deep mind and open space, interior and exterior, inside and outside, dandy and cowboy, East and West. Cather's novels fall, quite plainly, into two distinct groups: the urban novels and the prairie novels. Between them they form a familiar set of oppositions; within them, the oppositions are redoubled and openly dramatized. Before examining Cather's most remarkable novel, *The Professor's House* (1925)—a study of the interdependence of cowboy and dandy as real or lived mythologies—let us survey her career as a whole to see the extent to which our paradigm organizes it.

Although Cather's own notion of the relation between East and West in her work rests with the assertion that *My Ántonia* (1918) represents her triumph over the drawing-room preoccupations of Henry James (see "The Novel Démeublé" [1922a]), the relation between East and West in her novels is really a dialectical one. The structure is already in place in her first two books, *Alexander's Bridge* (1912) and *O Pioneers!* (1913). *Alexander's Bridge* is an urban, and extraordinarily urbane, work. Its protagonist, Bartley Alexander, lives in Boston, has lived in London, and was a student in Paris (1912, 26); his boyhood, however, was spent in the American West. *O Pioneers!*, by contrast, is a prairie novel par excellence (like *My Ántonia*, its ground is Cather's own girlhood Nebraska), and its protagonist, Alexandra Bergson (a female version of Alexander in both name and power, although psychologically also his opposite), is a prairie-bred farmowner despite her European birth. *The Song of the Lark* (1915) sounds like a prairie novel from its title, but the book itself is actually the narration of the title's movement as a trope from denotation to connotation. The lark is literal on the prairie, but figurative on the stage: Thea Kronborg, the novel's heroine, is a prairie girl who becomes an opera singer, moving from country to city as her career, like the novel itself, unfolds.

My Ántonia is, of course, Cather's most exemplary prairie novel, although Jim Burden, its narrator, has gone East to live after a plains childhood and adolescence, following his instructor at the University of Nebraska to Harvard to finish college (1918, 185). (In *A Lost Lady*, Niel attends the Massachusetts Institure of Technology [1923, 82].) As a boy, Burden reads a *Life of Jesse James* on his first journey West (a trip resembling Cather's own girlhood migration from Virginia to Nebraska), and he now returns to the frontier to narrate his own youth in the belatedness of retrospect. *Death Comes for the Archbishop* (1927)—along with *The Professor's House* Cather's most impressive spectrograph of the American Southwest—falls on the prairie side of the paradigm, although the novel begins with a meeting of Catholic prelates in Rome and maintains the magnificent irony throughout of a French priest, Latour, a meticulous aesthete, functioning as the seed of urbanity planted in the desert to make it bloom.

Cather's West is made meaningful—is made the West as such—by virtue of the oppositions that set it in relief. In *My Ántonia,* the young Western Burden memorizes *The Aeneid* in his upstairs study while "looking off at the distant river bluffs and the roll of the blond pastures between" (1918, 148). As a college freshman in Lincoln before his transfer East, his work table "looked out over the prairie" (1918, 166), while on the walls of his study there hangs "a large map of ancient Rome, the work of some German scholar" (1918, 166). The temporal structure of the novel as a whole is a crossing or metaleptic one: Jim remembers early by means of late ("images . . . that grew stronger with time" [1918, 226]), investing the prairie with the classical and biblical significations that make it fresh by virtue of comparisons with older things. In *Death Comes for the Archbishop,* the West is actually "an Indian Garden of Eden" (1927, 295). ("They longed," says Cather of her characters in *O Pioneers!,* "for a Jerusalem to deliver" [1913, 252].) The "great rock mesas" are, to Latour's eyes, "generally Gothic in outline" (1927, 94). Indeed, the "fluid" (1927, 96) look of the West renders it an overtly aesthetic field. Like the historian Turner's, Cather's Western landscape is a palimpsest as *My Ántonia* closes, and it "predetermines for us all that we can ever be" (1918, 238).

Cather even codes her use of proper names in relation to her customary oppositions. Latour's name and that of Jim Burden's tutor at the university in Lincoln, Gaston Cleric, between them form the name Gaston (de) Latour, the name of Pater's second-most famous imaginary hero and the subject of the longest of his imaginary portraits save that of Marius himself (Father Vaillant's brother in *Death Comes for the Archbishop* is actually named Marius [1927, 224], as is Sebastian's foster child in *Lucy Gayheart* [1935, 79]). And, like Pater's Marius, who has a "companion"—his "own proper self" (1885, 14, 256)—Alexander, too, has "a shadowy companion" in imagination, "his own young self" (1912, 40). Similarly, Emil Bergson, Alexandra's brother in *O Pioneers!* and a stranger to the frontier once he enters the university at Lincoln, unifies in his name Emil(e) Zola, the French novelist, and Henri Bergson, the French theoretician of temporality. And yet between them they form another familiar opposition, one between novelistic sociality and the philosophy of subjectivity, worlds presumably apart and yet, formally, the two literary poles between which Cather's own prose—like Virginia Woolf's—so vividly fluctuates.

The cleanliness of the oppositions—cowboy/dandy, prairie/ urban, country/city, nature/culture—always breaks down, testimony to the reciprocity or mutuality between them. In the prairie novels, for example, there are also dandies, and in the urban novels fugitives from the country are usually among the principal actors. In *O Pioneers!,* Frank Shabata, a Bohemian immigrant, sports rings, gloves, a fancy handkerchief, and a cane amid an agrarian community (he is also "melancholy and romantic" [1913, 144]), while in *A Lost Lady* Mrs. Forrester is celebrated amid a ranch community as a former urban sophisticate (she ends up in the cosmopolitan air of Buenos Aires at the story's close). Emil Bergson in *O Pioneers!* becomes a dressy college man but then goes on to visit Mexico as a cowboy adventurer; Carl Lindstrum, Alexandra's eventual mate in the novel, tries out both the city and Alaska, only to return home after dissatisfaction with both alternatives. Frank, of course, trades in the dandy's cane for the cowboy's Winchester rifle by the story's climax. If "the air and the earth are curiously mated and intermingled, as if the one were the breath of the other" (1913, 77), so the cowboy/dandy opposition is as a rule an interdependent one, too, dividing single characters as well as organizing patterns of distinction among groups of characters. The contrast or relief that structures Alexander's life, for example, is not a simple split between a Western boyhood and an Eastern career; as both a Western boy and a student in Paris, he looks both ways at once even from the start, at least the start as it emerges for him in the retrospect of reflection. *Lucy Gayheart* (1935), a late novel, also looks both ways at once, making Lucy a prairie girl who comes to Chicago and her teacher and lover Clement Sebastian a visiting European artist there. What is urban for one is frontier for the other. Like the prairie women's technique for sewing in *O Pioneers!*—a technique of "cross-stitch" (1913, 191)—Cather's writing willfully crosses over its own structures of assumption while also maintaining them. Indeed, it maintains them as a function of transgressing them.

CATHER'S WRITING IS ALREADY fully developed in *Alexander's Bridge* (1912), a remarkably wise and compact work for a first novel (the self-revisionary, Bloomian curiosities of Cather's dismissal of the book in a later preface to it suggest by negation just how paradigmatic it is [1922b]). It is worth reading closely before we turn at last to *The Professor's House*. The play or tension between our customary oppositions has an objective correlative in the suspension bridges that Alexander the architect builds, particularly the new, and unfinished, one at Moorlock that, like Alexander himself, experiences greater and greater strain as the story unwinds. Much as the Moorlock Bridge "is a continual anxiety" (1912, 5) to him because of its structural design, so, too, is the emotional strain on his constitution as the plot moves along. Although he comes to realize it only belatedly, he is suspended between cowboy and dandy, nature and culture: between a boyhood in "the rough days of the old West" (39) and an adult career in the East; between a former beloved in England and a wife in Boston now. The new bridge justly embodies both the structure of Alexander's feelings—indeed, of his psyche at large—and the structure of the novel's wider preoccupation with reciprocal, transgressive, crossing oppositions in a state of play.

The novel begins with a reversal: Wilson, Alexander's old philosophy professor from the unnamed Western university at which he studied as a young man, comes East to attend a congress of psychologists and to visit his old student in Boston. Emphasizing comparison or relief even in the novel's first chapter as a way to set things in motion, the narrator remarks, through the device of the professor's organizing consciousness, that the impressive Mrs. Alexander, with whom Wilson waits for Bartley to come home, is herself the function of a difference or opposition: "One immediately took for granted the costly privileges and fine spaces that must lie in the background from which such a figure could emerge with this rapid and elegant gait" (3). And yet when Bartley at last arrives, Mrs. Alexander jokingly describes him in terms that are just the reverse: "There he is. Away with perspective! No past, no future for Bartley; just the fiery moment" (8). However sardonic and estimable, Mrs. Alexander is blind to the structures that put her husband in place. Perspective is key rather than irrelevant.

And yet Bartley himself has the same blindness, at least early in the novel. "'You know how it is out West,'" he says. "'Old people are poked out of the way'" (11). The West is new, the East old; the West early, the East late. Like his wife, Alexander, too, confuses cause and effect. The belated, Romantic temporality of the West's settlement is what ironically secures its earliness. Sensitive to precisely this kind of irony, Cather accents the oddness of the teacher's coming from the West and the student's living in the East, even while the teacher nonetheless represents the learning ordinarily associated with the East and with Europe, and Alexander the student, urbanite though he is, represents a kind of raw cowboy energy, "rugged," "blond," and "six feet" tall (9). Despite Alexander's spontaneous energy, "the machinery was always pounding away in this man" (13), as if to suggest that, like his bridges, a structure must already be at work for his presumably spontaneous strength to function. As Cather puts it when Bartley feels excitement upon approaching England later in the novel, "he felt a sudden painful delight at being nearer another shore" (76)—a contrast, a difference, the crossing over to "another shore" that is needed to construct the kinds of oppositions from which sense, meaning, feeling are derived.

Part of Alexander's life machinery, too, is his near-forgotten love affair as a young man with the Irish actress Hilda Burgoyne. In decidedly formulaic fashion, Alexander meets Hilda while he is a student in Paris (26) and, quite accidentally, sees her perform again during his London trip, an experience that brings his old passion back to life, much to his own surprise. "He had not thought," says Cather, "of Hilda Burgoyne for years; indeed, he had almost forgotten her" (28) after meeting and marrying his wife Winifred. In recollection, Hilda, whom Bartley had not expected to become the success that she now is, combines, or is split by, the same kinds of contradictions that structure him: "that combination," as he puts it to himself, "of something homely and sensible, and something utterly wild and daft" (30). Cowboy and dandy, common sense and aestheticism, nature and culture—the same structures of opposition are already in place in Cather's first novel that her career will go on to elaborate and refine.

Nor is the play between past and present immune from representation. "The mummy room" at the British Museum had been "one of the chief delights" of Hilda's childhood (32), says Cather, a room in which "all the dead things in the world were assembled to make one's hour of youth the more precious" (33). The paradigm is both cultural and subjective. In a reflexive enactment of it, Cather paints London in decidedly Paterian terms, recognizable by trope, terms that emphasize relief, perspective, comparison as the central mechanisms of life: Alexander sees "Parliament catch fire with the sunset," "the slender tower . . . washed by a rain of golden light and licked by little flickering flames"; "the bleached gray pinnacles" even "floated in a luminous haze" (35). Indeed, the latter metaphor is the same Paterian one that Woolf uses in "Modern Fiction" to describe life itself—"a luminous halo" (1919, 2:106). No wonder the stirrings of past love reawaken in Alexander only after his return home to Boston, including "the vibration of an unnatural excitement" and "a sense of quickened life" (68).

But Alexander cannot handle the new awareness brought on by the heightened role—and rule—of contrasts. So concerned does he grow about the tensions that structure him that he eventually gives their effects plain voice: "'I am never at peace,'" he says in a letter to Hilda; "'I feel always on the edge of danger and change'" (101). And yet the "edge" is just another figure for Paterian relief or crossing over, the structure necessary to give anything and everything its contours despite the pain it may cause. Although "'it seems,'" he writes, "'that a man is meant to live only one life in this world'" (102), and that "'when he tries to live a second he develops another nature'" (102), it is not a question of choice at all. Two natures have already structured his life, even before he meets Hilda as a student: his life on the range in one part of his youth, his life as a student in Paris in another. He has acknowledged that life is a "patchwork" (70). But however inevitable its splits or tensions may be, Bartley finds being too conscious of them, particularly of the youthfulness reawakened by his love for Hilda, insupportable. "It was," says the narrator, remarking on his obsession with her, "impossible to live like this any longer" (114).

Simultaneous with Alexander's increasing nervous strain is the straining of the cantilever bridge still under construction at Moorlock, already famous as the biggest such bridge in the world. Like Alexander himself, "the lower chords" of the bridge, so reports indicate, are "showing strain" (121), much as the "lower" or deeper "chords" in his own nature are "showing strain" emotionally. The bridge does indeed snap (124), throwing Alexander and everyone else at the site into the cold water beneath it. Alexander is "a strong swimmer" (126), but he drowns anyway. Like the bridge, he, too, needs "another shore," but as the bridge's own difficulties show, such a structure collapses when a tension of opposites is strain rather than support. It is support that Cather goes on to find in *The Professor's House.*

THE PROFESSOR'S HOUSE (1925) not only formalizes the relation between the cowboy and the dandy in American culture; it also perfects conceptual organization in Cather's fiction, distributing with the least residue and uncleanliness or crossover in her novels (there is some irony in this) the component elements of her writing that in *Alexander's Bridge,* for example, or in *O Pioneers!* are less plainly schematic than they are here. Like Emerson, Cather shows the West to be a projection of earlier influences from the East and from Europe. And, like Pater, she thematizes the play of these boundaries as they fashion what Emersonian world there is to represent. Cather also reminds us with special and summary clarity in *The Professor's House* that West and East are the master tropes for what we have called the cowboy and the dandy, prairie and urbanity, nature and culture, outside and inside, open space and deep mind. The Western journey out and the aesthetic journey within are parallel. By virtue of a provocative error in *The Armies of the Night* (1968), Mailer even shows how close these histories are by assigning to Emerson rather than to Pater the phrase "hard gemlike flame" (1968, 44).

Our structures of opposition are effective in *The Professor's House* not just from the narrative's point of view but from those of its characters as well. Mythologies, like religious beliefs, are the very stuff of lived experience. Much as Puccini composes both *La Bohème* (1896) and *La fanciulla del West* (1910), Cather joins—"conjoins" is more appropriate, since she shows the relation to be the function of a difference—Professor Godfrey St. Peter, a historian and American aesthete, with his student and friend, Tom Outland, a real, and self-conscious, cowboy.

Although an American "born on Lake Michigan" (1925, 12), the professor is also an old dandy whose student days were passed in France. "He had spent the happiest years of his youth," says Cather, "in a house at Versailles" (12). Like his first name—Napoleon—his last name suggests, of course, an institutionalizing power: he is rock or ground, while his foil, Tom, is a nomad. But then again, Bonaparte was a Corsican corporal, and St. Peter's students call him "Mephistopheles" (13), his sleek and sophisticated look suggesting, as that of all aesthetes should, the figure of a Miltonic Satan. "He kindled" when delighted (28), Cather tells us, assuring us that his aesthetic legacy is Pater's by way of exact tropological allusion. Not only that; he is a historian of the Spanish adventurers who preceded both the French and the English in North America (16), a scholar, as it were, of the precursor. And yet the professor also partakes of the other side—the cowboy side—of the opposition that defines him. He is, like Alexander, "a tireless swimmer" (12), a man who "saunter[s]" when he walks (54), a man who wears "a Stetson hat" when he works in his beloved garden (112). And yet, unlike Alexander, he is able to stay afloat in a world that combines East and West, dandy and cowboy, culture and nature.

Tom Outland is, by contrast, a genuine Westerner, a bona fide cowboy, complete with his own Stetson hat when he first visits the professor as a prospective student at the midwestern university at which St. Peter teaches. Nor is Tom just a cowpuncher; reflecting the book's own double stance, he is also a scientist who invents a revolutionary airplane engine and a reader of Virgil in Latin, thanks to a Spanish priest who once tutored him in New Mexico. Also an explorer, Tom has discovered, as the saying goes, an abandoned pueblo city whose architecture recalls the Shelleyan paradigm from which it must nonetheless diverge so as to be Native American, an irony that the novel mines deeply, as it were, and with enormous delight. In the very heart of the country, the city already has its shrine. Tom's diary, describing what he calls Cliff City—the whole of the novel's second section—emphasizes the reciprocity rather than the opposition between East and West, Europe and America, urban and prairie. The ancient ruins that Tom discovers are first seen as a "skyline" (191). The city also has a "round tower" (201), the visionary site proper, English Romantic style, here in this remote and abandoned place. "I'd never seen a tower like that one," writes Tom (203). "It seemed to me to mark a difference" (203).

Of course it does. Difference or relief is the design of both Cather's writing and her characters' experience. Tom's first night on the mesa prompts "a religious emotion" (251), although one borrowed from European learning, an emotion that structures the spot with a significance it presumably lacked before: "I had read of filial piety in the Latin poets," he writes, "and I knew that was what I felt for this place" (251). The irony of prior, European influence investing these ruins with meaning is, however, repressed in Tom's mind at the very moment that the double movement plain to us occurs: "my happiness," he writes at the conclusion of the passage that invokes "the Latin poets," "was unalloyed" (251). What impresses Father Duchene, the priest whom Tom asks to inspect Cliff City with him after he has settled it, is something similar: that the extinct tribe that built it had worked, or so it seems, "without . . . influence" (221). "When I look into the *Aeneid* now," says a franker Tom a bit later on, recalling Jim Burden in his study, "I can always see two pictures: the one on the page, and another behind that: blue and purple rocks . . . a rude tower rising . . . a dark grotto" (253). The two sites make each other live. "The unassisted eye" (218), Tom realizes, now seeing the whole design, is helpless.

Perhaps Tom's story is outlandish. Cather herself calls it "fantastic" at the beginning of the novel's third and last section (257). Meanwhile, the professor praises Tom's diary in the Paterian terms we come to expect from him, pointing out the tact of omission—the *ascesis*—that it shows in its deceptively plain style (262) and concluding that Tom's imagination is a "kindling one" (262). Part "outlaw," part "land," Tom Outland's name alone is obviously enough to suggest the familiar cowboy paradox of the loner hero, the outlaw actually serving land and law by transgressing their authority—a description fair to Tom himself and also a superb instance of the enabling transgressions common to English and American Romanticism alike. Both cowboys and dandies *are* "outlandish" (43)—Cather goes ahead and uses the word. Both, after all, are uneasy with boundaries although in different ways. Tom's West emerges by contrast with the professor's Europe, even though West and East are also tainted by one another. Whether image, notion, or experience, each needs the other to be what it is.

7

MILES APART?

Miles Davis remains the consummate portrait of black urbanity that we have. His fiercely agonistic relation to Louis Armstrong structures his career and explains the relation of jazz modernism, whether bop or rock, to early jazz itself. If Armstrong crosses from country to city like a jazz Moses, then Davis's reaction to all that Armstrong represents—the full, open tone, the exuberance, the primacy—is a crossing back, a revisionary, urban curtailment of the enthusiasm of the South. Here bop and rock and roll impulses join under the common banner of a jazz modernism that, in two very different ways, revises the country fullness of the whole history of jazz in its days of enthusiasm from Dixieland to swing. Davis's controversial turn to a rock mode in the late 1960s is an entirely natural one, since it has in common with the bop mode of his youth the intervention by the city in the country's presumption of knowing ways. Let us consider Davis's relation to Armstrong before surveying the movement of his career.

Armstrong oppresses Davis as both a musician and a performer, especially with his grinning and "acting the clown," as Davis describes it in his autobiography (1989, 83). And yet, he says, "you can't play nothing on trumpet that doesn't come from him, not even modern shit" (316). Davis's "whole view of himself and his function," writes Ian Carr, "was totally opposite to that of Armstrong" (1982, 117), even though—perhaps because—it is with Armstrong that his principal relation is to be found. Armstrong is the only sufficiently absolute master with whom a musician as absolute as Davis himself might presume to draw comparisons. Besides, all earlier trumpet players are themselves decisively indebted to Armstrong, prompting an ambition in Davis appropriate to his desire to seek tradition out at its source. Like his early relation to Clark Terry (see Cole 1974, 37; Carr 1982, 88), his relation to Dizzy Gillespie is largely inconsequential compared to the relation to Armstrong, not just because it comes relatively late in his youth but also because he surpasses Dizzy at his own game in quality of fast licks, quality of blues feeling, and use of the mute. Indeed, both also have a self-conscious precursor in Roy Eldridge (Gitler 1985, 56; Davis 1989, 8), suggesting an earlier, more genuinely common precursor for both in Armstrong himself.

The central principle of Davis's career is a moderation of the naturalness of breath represented by Armstrong's full, open, lyrical trumpet. It emphasizes breath's construction through tone, shade, and grain, even if it requires a distortion of Armstrong's precise strength in order to do so. Darkening the country optimism of the precursor, Davis debunks Armstrong's exuberance, a hot openness that is wiser, more appropriate when it is transformed into urban cool. Jack Chambers notes that Elwood Buchanan, Davis's first teacher in St. Louis, had already steered him away from Armstrong in favor of a "lighter tone without vibrato" (1983, 10, 11), a predisposition that also well suited the young prodigy's familiarity with classical tone.

Davis does indeed classicize Armstrong's instrument (he came to New York from St. Louis at the age of seventeen to attend Juilliard), presumably revivifying it under new terms but really returning it, via the grainy tone and the mute, to its originary ground of struggle with earlier traditions of determination long repressed by Armstrong's own success, including the classical itself. While Armstrong's early Dixieland style gives way to a trifle mellower sound when larger bands kick Dixieland into plainer swing grooves as the Twenties give way to the Thirties, the exuberance of Armstrong's horn, its open tonality, actually grows even bolder, perhaps because of the new instrumention. Much as the backbeat later on reimagines the sound of marching band drums, Armstrong had already turned a trick by converting the trumpet, instrument of imperial triumph and oppression, into one of African-American celebration. Armstrong's joy comes from bending the oppressor's instrument of rule, the bugle, the military marching band instrument par excellence, into its precise opposite, an instrument of jubilation in the hands of the oppressed. Early in his career, Armstrong's first brass instrument was literally a bugle (Jones and Chilton 1971, 13), after which he switched to cornet, then to trumpet in 1926 (Collier 1983, 162; recall, too, that Armstrong had been in a military-style waifs' home as a boy; see Giddins 1988, 65 ff.). The wit alone is enough to infuriate the otherwise grateful latecomer, who is left with nothing but a sub-jection of his own to the dominant trumpet form handed down to him.

Hence the necessity of Davis's misreading of Armstrong: to take away the culture of Armstrong's invention and misrepresent it as a dull force of nature. But Armstrong's own country or Southern natu-ralness, of course, is itself a myth. Bitter at its sound, Davis qualifies it in the sophisticated hindsight of his own ultimate urbanity. He swerves from, outpowers his anxious enablement by Armstrong by calling Armstrong's exuberance into question, suggesting that such vitality must really be the sign of something else, in this case the mimicry particular to the colonial subjection that Davis, apparently unlike Armstrong himself, will resist. He not only forces Armstrong to look like a bugler; he also enlists the classical in the evolution of a postclassical form, subduing both Armstrong and classical at the same time by setting them off against one another. The swing trum-pet that intervenes between Davis and Armstrong chronologically only exacerbates for Davis what is already problematic in Armstrong himself—too great an openness, even if Armstrong's openness, like Toni Morrison's re-membering, is really a self-conscious myth. If Armstrong's exuberance is the result of a struggle with Sousa, then Davis's is the ironic result of a struggle with the exuberance gained from it. His is a stringent secularity that deracinates everything, ac-cepting, in postmodern fashion, the rule of contrasts that shapes what world there is. Why does Davis supersede even Gillespie as the public emblem for the hipster who wears sunglasses at night? Be-cause sunglasses at night, cool and urban, heighten, like his music, the sense of all things as artifice, labor, construction, rendering both world and self more deliberately aesthetic.

There is, of course, an additional irony at work beyond Davis's misrepresentation of Armstrong. The extreme lyricism of Arm-strong's own horn has a Davis kind of fillip in it: his exuberance on his instrument is actually more vocal, more lyrical than his voice; his grainy voice, meanwhile, is more instrumental than his instrument. The crossing structure of the relation between Armstrong's voice and horn—I have already alluded to it in the introduction—is one that shows black urbanity's full hand at the origin, as it were, of its own history: Armstrong's self-invention is already premised on the abrogation of voice's primacy by the instrument, this achievement the ironic yield of bringing country usages to city modes. When in 1956, for example, Armstrong records an album with Ella Fitzgerald, the purest of all jazz singers, the contrast between them makes Armstrong's own self-defining contrasts even plainer.

Achieved as Armstrong's naturalness is, then, it is for Davis an endlessly galling precedent. Thus his first target of deracination is as a rule the instrument itself. For Davis, the horn is not, as it seems to be for Armstrong (although this is Davis's myth of Armstrong), a happy transcription of voice; its tone is really nothing but grain, shadow, relief, always the function of a relation to something purer—Armstrong himself—that is present but unspoken. Davis's characteristic use of the mute makes the revisionary relation especially clear, almost literal, in suppressing the vitality of Armstrong's very sound, building a resistance to its texture, and changing our notion of trumpet itself as he transforms Armstrong's blaze into his own darker flame.

DAVIS'S EARLY DAYS AS group leader begin after he leaves Parker's quintet at Christmas 1948 (Gitler 1985, 219). In 1949, *The Birth of the Cool* establishes his customary sound and stance as a leader in his own right, a sound and stance distinguished by the emergence of the almost Western spatiality of the long tones that start to preoccupy his phrasing in the period which follows his youth as Parker's fast-phrasing sideman and prefigures crucial aspects of the later rock mode. By the mid-Fifties, Davis is already the very center of jazz, postdating Parker and both predating and, as it turns out, postdating John Coltrane, too, one of Parker's few genuine peers in influence in the history of saxophone. Let us read some of Davis's tunes from the Fifties, culminating with "So What" on the legendary *Kind of Blue* in 1959, before turning to his continuing changes through the Sixties.

Two tunes from a November 1955 session released under the title *Miles* well represent the clarity of structure that connects the early Davis with the late and that also informs the unity, as it were, of given performances. The relation to Armstrong is as a rule the most striking example of it. "Just Squeeze Me," a cover of a Duke Ellington and Lee Gaines composition, suggests even in its title (fortuitously, of course) the difference between Davis's and Armstrong's stances—the grainy elasticity or porousness of Davis's sound as opposed to the hard if bouncy fullness of Armstrong's. A ballad sped up a bit, the tune resists swing styles in Davis's breathy, slow-down-and-kiss-me articulation of the head. While Davis's decisive reimagination of the mute is part of the revision of Armstrong's earlier stomping sound, the fact that one cannot always tell whether the mute is actually on or not is proof that the contraction of Armstrong's openness proceeds from the lip rather than from the mute itself. Against Red Garland's swinging piano, Davis's own new, ascetic lyricism moves beyond bop's sixteenth-note protocols toward a postmodern jazz minimalism, for which he deserves much of the credit. The strategic hesitation with which he rolls up a scale into his solo is both disturbing and refreshing. It is, of course, the long tones that dominate the phrasing, its spacings borrowed from Armstrong but reimagined through the different tone and attack available to Davis from his classical schooling. Davis sucks as much air out of the horn as Armstrong breathes into it. Within the solo itself, however, another residual style can also be heard, however occasionally, with which Davis crosses the breathlessness—the withering assault on a chord, using the gruppetti, for example, so adored by Parkerites, to restore blues feeling to the bleak terrain. Coltrane's solo dramatizes his own struggle with Parker as he tries to outmanuever the gruppetto as a device. Davis ends the song with a series of unexpectedly lyrical phrases that join with Coltrane's long tones to summarize the crossing strains in the tune as a whole.

On a swinging tune like "The Theme" (Davis takes credit for its composition although it derives from a Thelonious Monk composition known as "The Fifty-second Street Theme"), the crossing paradigm emerges in a different way, using different materials. Indeed, as a jamming structure, it previews a relation between jazz and rock and roll that exceeds the relation between Davis and rock alone. The logic of the tune's very conception is actually a rhythm and blues one in its use of octave dropping as a melodic device both in the head and during the only half-improvised exchange between Davis and Coltrane in the vamp toward tune's end. In fact, the head is hardly a head at all, just a series of riffs. With the proleptic appeal of a later r & b standard like Steve Cropper and Don Covay's 1965 "Seesaw," for example (covered by Aretha Franklin in 1968), "The Theme" uses octave devices to structure the tune as a whole and to inform the solos. Davis's solo counterpoints bop and rhythm and blues as historically combustible idioms, putting them at last in dialogue or conversation. Even Coltrane waxes surprisingly funky at the start of his solo before rifling through the bop influences that begin suddenly to oppress him in the middle of his blue celebration. By the solo's second half, he has found his compromise ground between the alternatives of the blues as such and simply the shredding of scales. While "The Theme" ends with the necessity of repeating the head, it does so only once, with a bit of defiance accompanying the brevity with which the head proper, unlike the luxurious octave vamps, concludes.

Davis's most durable single album, of course, is *Kind of Blue* (1959). The fact alone that Cannonball Adderley and John Coltrane can perform together so smoothly given their divergent paths later on is testimony to the coordination (not synthesis) of the sounds created, a coordination of vocabularies of the kind already adumbrated as a Davis-band trademark in 1955 (the hard bop fusion represented by Adderley here—the fusion of bop melodics over funky grooves associated with Horace Silver in particular—has a very real and assured mode of success until the late 1960s, when the attempt to satisfy two masters at the same time becomes too difficult to maintain). "So What," a modal composition written (or, really, structured) by Davis himself, is the album's most memorable tune and one that well exemplifies both the session's project and the larger crossings to which we have been attentive. Here the simplicity of swing riffs crosses with the sophistication of modal changes to produce an overt play between country and city, cowboy and dandy. Despite its harmonically advanced opening, "So What" is reminiscent of the secondary strategy of "The Theme"—a riff as the theme, an old swing device and one surprisingly still alive among the highest of young jazz sensibilities in 1959. The use of bass to tell the melody sounds like a radically rock concept well before the fact, but then again, perhaps the rock concept is a belated repetition of an older jazz strategy.

When Davis's solo begins, what is his first move? On this decidedly swinging tune, he waits. Not only is there a space of self-consciousness created in relation to time; he also acknowledges his belatedness in a readily dramatic way that informs the very logic of his phrasing. Waiting is another definition of the cool, an infinite stoicism given the inevitability of distance from the primacy represented by Armstrong in particular. Occasionally Davis almost spits, delicately, into the horn, arresting any strong propensity for openness to which the horn he blows is historically sensitive, remaking it as an instrument with a use of breath altogether different from Armstrong's own. Spatializing, simplifying over the tune's swinging groove, the solo's construction walks a remarkably tight line—negotiates an edge or precipice—between shouting blues and absolute cool, a balance of South and North, country and city, cowboy and dandy, a conversation of the two modes whose crossing makes up Davis's persona (Coltrane follows by requiring even starker poems, seeking his own swerve from High Bop).

Adderley's presence (his solo follows Coltrane's) remains an oddity despite its perfection. In fact, it is its perfection that is odd. Its ease within a largely single vocabulary, however genuinely synthetic, contrasts with Davis's and Coltrane's acting out and working through of the kinds of crossings with which we are familiar. If Adderley shows us anything on *Kind of Blue,* it is that hard bop, despites its deliciousness, was finally a holding action against the choice between the avant-garde and the rock mode that divided jazz all over again in the late 1960s in a manner reminiscent of its earlier division into bop and rhythm and blues after the swing era.

Davis's George Coleman group, however, is a step backward, although its regressiveness is leavened on an album like *Seven Steps to Heaven* (1963) by a new pianist, the young Herbie Hancock, who makes up for Coleman's lack of focus by installing a new kind of difference in Davis's sound. If "Just Squeeze Me" is a cool Davis and "So What" a balanced one, here the fast is as a rule simply faster, a throwback to Parker strategies, a transitory weak phase in Davis's career exemplified, and perhaps abetted, by Coleman himself, tenorman with Davis from 1963 to 1964 and finally a journeyman, lightning fast and sometimes soulful but with little of the agonistic originality of Davis's hornmen before and after him. The band on *Seven Steps to Heaven* is nonetheless fresh, thanks to Hancock's rhythm and blues chordings. Designed to bolster heads and solos, they also contrast with the bop speediness of the horn improvisations and so provide the kind of crossing at an ensemble level usually to be found in the construction of Davis's solos. Here, however, even Davis's solos are, like Coleman's, very often throwbacks to bop exhibitionism, although Hancock's extraordinary rhythmic fluidity makes up for Davis and Coleman alike by opening greater spaces in the ensemble sound that prefigure the next—and still controversial—phase of Davis's career.

Miles in the Sky (1968), Davis's first fully backbeated recording, is the beginning of his rock phase and the recording that makes this otherwise notorious turn altogether logical from the point of view of his earlier development. Hancock's opening riffs on "Stuff," the album's first tune, are both genuinely funky and genuinely sophisticated, suggesting a crossing strategy in the sound's conception that is more than a commercial one. A Davis composition, the tune's horn head begins uptight, then relaxes, crossing back and forth between the two stances in a rhythm of difference that garners strength and density from the repetition of the contrast between them. The horns even show a note of surprise at discovering this regularity just before the solos begin, which, not surprisingly, take a very long time to come. As a soloist, Davis recapitulates the crossings in the head by shifting back and forth from glory to grain—from Armstrong to his revision of Armstrong—strategically weighing the two tonalities against each other in a mode of comparison that structures the double stance of his rock phase as a whole and that actually hyperbolizes the split structure of his stance as we have sketched it from the beginning of his career till now. Proving that the rigors of his central period apply as well to the rockophile, he is at last having an overt conversation with Armstrong himself, perhaps because of the freedom from the very institution of jazz that the switch to the backbeat allows.

In a Silent Way (1969) is also a manifest elaboration of Davis's earlier work, the electric counterpart to Gil Evans collaborations like *Sketches of Spain* (1960) and his version of the replacement of reeds by guitar. The cool tone poem has now been refined to such a degree that the very structure of swinging itself has, astonishingly enough, been revised. Davis's propensity for phrasing backwards as a bopper now converges with his propensity for silence as a tone poet. Here the cool finally meets the backbeat face to face. The result is a new curtailment of the soloing instrument as such. The needs common to both legacies of swing, the cool and the funky, the bop and the r & b, find a place to meet beyond the plainer synthetics of hard bop. Not surprisingly, it is Hancock who is the medium through which Davis negotiates these crossings as an ensemblist. Here the piano is both vigorously rhythmic and vigorously lyrical, the secure double ground of the entire album. What expectations may be left unfulfilled by Davis's own soloing are compensated for by Hancock's rhythmic lyricism as soloist and accompanist alike. In fact, there are, in the normal sense, no solos at all on *In a Silent Way*. The virtual transformation of soloing as a category leads to a new group principle here and on *Bitches Brew* (1970), one that rotates, finally, on Hancock's endless crossing between the lyrical and the rhythmic, a crossing that transfers Davis's customary self-division as a soloist onto the sound of the ensemble as a whole.

However thoughtless or superb his progeny may be (bop's heirs could be thoughtless, too), Davis fashions the paradigm and provides the authority for a crossover stance that remains both durable and controversial. To describe it as a crossing of jazz and rock, however, is less accurate than to describe it as a crossing of two jazz modes—one cool, one funky—that between them structure what is now a common path away from bop's influence beyond hard bop. Like the backbeat, Davis's cool is, after all, an alternative to bop, too, and joins with it in a double effort to modulate the history of jazz itself into the history of rock and roll. Because he has already met Armstrong at the crossroads, Davis can cross back to the country, the South, the backbeat, without risking a return to enthusiasm.

8

VIRGINIA WOOLF'S CROSSWRITING

M uch as rhythm and blues is the link between jazz and rock and roll, aestheticism is the link between Romanticism and literary modernism. Willa Cather's English contemporary and soulmate, Virginia Woolf, is a more recognizably Paterian figure than Cather herself, and one who focuses throughout her work on the interdependence of nature and culture that the mythologies of the cowboy and the dandy represent in Cather's own novels. If the bohemian urbanity that Woolf and Cather share is biographically manifest—Cather in Greenwich Village, Woolf in Bloomsbury—so, too, are their tropological similarities from the point of view of Romantic tradition proper. Just as Cather paints the mind through metaphors of landscape, Woolf customarily represents the inside by means of the outside. Thinking of Mrs. Forrester's impressiveness in *A Lost Lady* (1923), Niel, Cather's narrator, looks "exultantly into the streak of red sunset" (1923, 31). Here the seemingly simple rhetoric simultaneously represents Niel's joy in beholding Mrs. Forrester ("exultantly") while also prefiguring his imminent disillusion regarding her ("sunset"), picturing his feelings by virtue of a relation to a world outside himself. Similarly, Woolf: "Down his mind went," she writes of Peter Walsh in *Mrs. Dalloway,* "flat as a marsh" (1925, 78). Especially in the London setting, Woolf's Romanticism—the construction of a difference between inside and outside based, ironically, on their exchange or identity—emerges in high relief. In both cases, in Cather's a bit more literally perhaps, landscape is the correlative for a state of mind and the precise vehicle for its description. As in "Mont Blanc," the inside exists—can exist—only in relation to an outside from which it is different.

Thus Woolf's characteristic late Romantic inwardness, fed by her relation to Henry James as well as to Pater, is, like Cather's outlandishness, really a dialectic between inside and outside, the function of an exchange or crossing between the social and the psychological that fashions world and subjects alike from the ground up. Woolf's language doesn't just record this crossing; it performs it. It is a very particular mode of active writing in which rival or contradictory assumptions can coexist with ease despite—perhaps because of—the differences out of which they are made. In her essays, the stance is present from the very beginning and is dramatized by a dialogical procedure in which Woolf often addresses her reader before turning back on what she has said to revise her own assumptions, a procedure won, as Beth Rosenberg has suggested, by virtue of a dialogue with Samuel Johnson (1995). Let us see how this achievement unfolds in Woolf's fiction as she both deploys and interrogates the category of inwardness over the course of her career as a novelist. In the posthumous *Between the Acts* (1941)—our discussion will conclude with it—she actually undoes the difference between inside and outside by showing how reciprocal they are, this after a whole career spent perfecting the representation of the presumably absolute difference between them. The creation of interiority, of a distinction between an inside and an outside upon which the conviction of a deep subjectivity rests, is, as everyone knows, the emergent project of Woolf's first three novels: *The Voyage Out* (1915) and its visionary lyricism; *Night and Day* (1919) and its flight from an inwardness whose appeal nonetheless suffuses what is otherwise a rather conventional Edwardian novel of manners; and *Jacob's Room* (1922), the moment, to use Philip Roth's phrase, of Woolf's letting go of convention and allowing an apparently given interiority in character to speak.

It is not, however, until *Mrs. Dalloway* (1925) that Woolf fully constructs her poetics of inwardness, presenting there a conception of the psyche based upon categories of inside and outside that the relation between Septimus and Clarissa helps to structure as the novel moves along. Indeed, Septimus and Clarissa, particularly with Woolf's own belated recommendation in her introduction to the 1928 Modern Library edition of the novel that we read them as "double[s]" (1928b, vi), are probably the most axiomatic representatives of the dichotomies that structure Woolf's notion of subjectivity, dichotomies whose ideal destiny is the picture of a unified or synthetic psyche.

How many dichotomies do Clarissa and Septimus represent? The list is legion. Septimus is all outside, Clarissa is all inside; each suffers from the lack of the other. Because of war trauma, he cannot manage to establish a proper boundary—a proper ego—between his own impressions and those outside him; she, by contrast, fears the outside too much, retreating into perhaps too sharply defined an inside for her own good. Septimus is, to use Jacques Lacan's phrase, the body in pieces, the fragmentation away from which the ego turns in order to put itself in place; Clarissa, by contrast, is reasonably stable, although the effort to be so is always manifest: "That was her self—pointed; dartlike; definite. That was her self when some effort, some call on her to be her self, drew the parts together, she alone knew now different, how incompatible, and composed so for the world only into one center" (1925, 55). If you put Clarissa and Septimus together, you a get a whole or integrated personality. In *To the Lighthouse* (1927), Mr. and Mrs. Ramsay also form between them the poles of an ideal fusion or harmony, although Woolf's doubts about the givenness of the subjectivity that family romance presumably bestows is also manifest there.

Orlando (1928), the novel that directly follows *To the Lighthouse,* is, on the one hand, the perfect continuation of this movement in Woolf's career—Orlando's androgyny is the surpassing testimony to the conviction of a deep subjectivity or interiority in all of Woolf's fiction, since Orlando's character remains the same despite the vicissitudes of society and history, and despite the otherwise decisive determinant of subjectivity, gender, which, of course, changes midway through the book (1928a, 137). On the other hand, *Orlando* is also a text that radically criticizes the very notion of innate subjectivity that appears to be its principal assumption, since it goes out of its way to insist upon the determinations of history, culture, and the social assignment of gender in the production of human subjectivity. "It is clothes that wear us," Woolf reminds us, "and not we them" (188). By switching Orlando's gender as she does, Woolf simultaneously preserves and cancels any notion of Orlando's character as a given. The rival demands of soul and history struggle beneath the luxury of both the plot and Woolf's apparently seamless language here at the chronological center of her career as a novelist.

Even the book's rhetoric operates in a double or self-contradictory way. If "openness," for example, "was the soul" of Orlando's "nature" (189), then the outside, "openness," and the inside, "soul," are perilously, and curiously, identified. "Everything, in fact," as Woolf puts it in the novel's third chapter, "was something else" (143). How can what is "in fact" be "something else"? By definition, a "fact" is what it is, but here, quite ironically, the self-evidence of "fact" is represented as "something else." As with Shelley, form comes into being only in relief, as the function of a relation to or a difference from something else. Everything in *Orlando* is as a rule put into place by its transgression, this as a specific and exact rhetorical strategy on Woolf's part, a strategy of crossing over. The seeming imprecision in Woolf's language is really a principal pattern throughout the novel. It is the key not only to its rhetorical structure but also to its own estimation of representational categories such as fact and fiction, text and world, one gender and another, and, of course, inside and outside. When we are told at the moment of Orlando's change of gender that "he was a woman" (137), assumption is transgressed before the sentence can even be completed. But the change slides over us as entirely natural. We understand the sentence without a hitch. And when we enter at last upon the present at the book's close, the necessities of language require another hyperbolic instance of the same crossing rhetoric at work throughout the story: "It was," says the narrator in the past tense, "the present moment" (298). The active logic of Woolf's writing in *Orlando* calls into question the very categories that also organize it.

This strategy or procedure is, to coin a term, Woolf's crosswriting—the transgression or crossing over of one's own assumptions even as they are put into place. Crossover rhetoric is a kind of sleight-of-hand whose mechanisms are everywhere in *Orlando* itself. "The most poetic" kind of "conversation," says Woolf, "is precisely that which cannot be written down" (1928a, 253). This creates not simply belief on the reader's part in the depth of the conversation so described—here a conversation between Orlando and Shelmerdine—but also the belief that such "repletion," as she puts it, such fullness of feeling, can be the effect of "a great blank" (253). Even the opposition between life and literature is handled—is simultaneously established and erased—by crossover rhetoric. While life and literature are on the one hand distinct—"Green in nature is one thing, green in literature another"(18)—on the other hand they are not: the queen "read him" (Orlando) "like a page" (25). Not only, of course, because Orlando is a page to the court, but also because the continuity between life and literature is, as the book's whole ambience suggests anyway, to be emphasized simultaneously with its insistence that there is no continuity between them at all. "A page torn from the thickest volume of human life" (222), says an endlessly crossing Woolf, is more "absorbing" than "any play" (222). At one and the same time, a distinction between life and literature is drawn by terms that compare them.

THE SELF-REVISIONARY stance that Woolf takes in *Orlando* in relation to her own presumably given categories, particularly the givenness of subjectivity, is a new, emerging pattern as her fiction moves into its later phase. If *The Waves* (1931) reifies interiority, then *The Years* (1937) ossifies historical or external determination. *Between the Acts* (1941), however, is Woolf's consummately self-revisionary text, plainly using and disrupting at the same time the kind of psychological representation for which we customarily celebrate her.

How does Woolf's crosswriting work in *Between the Acts*? Like *Orlando, Between the Acts* is a more compelling novel today than it was, say, ten or twenty years ago. Magic realism has belatedly canonized *Orlando* and made it the new center of Woolf's fiction (see, for example, Barr 1992) now that *Mrs. Dalloway* and *To the Lighthouse* are the models for what is really a waning psychological realism in the present history of the novel. We can reinvent our view of *Between the Acts,* too, as the likely inauguration of English postmodernism, this from the woman who, twenty years before, had embodied High Modernism in England. *Between the Acts* both repeats and rejects the representational categories developed over the course of her career. It summarizes the achievement of the distinction between inside and outside while also collapsing it.

Between the Acts is a manifestly boundary-crossing text, a book virtually consumed by dialogue running over itself, like a Robert Altman film; it also takes the crosswriting project of *Orlando* a step further. *Orlando*'s rhetorical strategy becomes an overtly thematic one in *Between the Acts*. If the opposition that structures *Orlando* is one between the sexes, then the opposition that structures *Between the Acts* is one between inside and outside. Woolf's last novel is actually her most radical one, since, by virtue of her crosswriting, it not only articulates but also breaks apart the opposition most dear to us, most natural, most Woolfian—the opposition between self and world. Of course, as a paradigm it is the same opposition as that between the genders, but what is at stake now is the basic opposition that puts the world in place in the first place, even before (should we like to use a psychoanalytic model) the emergence of gender distinctions. The distinction between inside and outside upon which gender differences are themselves propped is the most elementary of structuring necessities required to guarantee the very existence of a psyche, of an inwardness that, after modernism anyway, we too often take for granted as already there.

By staging a play—a pageant—within its representation of English village life, *Between the Acts* sets up a distinction between the real and the represented that it simultaneously erases and preserves. Indeed, it breaks down the opposition between world and representation by means of putting it in place. What is remarkable about the novel's story is that the confusion between what is inside and what is outside—what is in the head and what is on stage—grows more and more problematic as the text moves along. It even becomes the subject of discussion. "'Did she mean,'" says someone about Miss La Trobe, the pageant's author, "'something hidden,'" something "'unconscious?'" (1941, 199). Maybe. "'He said she meant we all act. Yes, but whose play?'" (199–200). Hence *Between the Acts* well conveys what interpreters do when trying to reduce a text (in this case the pageant): they become part of a pageant, too, an interpretative one continuous with rather than distinct from the text to be interpreted and sharing in its myths and assumptions.

Early in the novel, Woolf calls blunt attention to the questions at hand. When Giles Oliver comes home to find guests at the house, he retires to his room to change and to reflect, and to prompt a remarkably unlikely trope from the narrator. "The ghost of convention," says Woolf, "rose to the surface" (46). For good Woolfians, "convention" is the surface, and what Woolf characteristically does is to strip convention away to get at the "deep centre" (44) of life, as she calls it here. But now Woolf has made an incredible and irreparable change in point of view: what is deep is convention itself. Convention structures what we may at least in passing call the unconscious. Such a new understanding of the self begins to undo what seem to be Woolf's customary coordinates of inside and outside. Woolf even has Giles and his wife, Isa, recite some lines from Keats in order to speak to one another (64). Old Bart Oliver wonders whether or not—he believes not—there can be, as he puts it, "'thoughts without words'" (55). "'Quite beyond me,'" replies Mrs. Manresa, one of the guests, making the point by virtue of the negation that constitutes it. "A thread united them," says Woolf, "visible, invisible" (55)—the "thread" of "convention," including language and its rules.

How does the novel pursue this reversal of modernist assumption in its sustained revision of Woolf's entire career? By staging Miss La Trobe's pageant, with all its mechanisms in full, almost Brechtian view, and by staging the audience's problematic relation to what, at least by normative assumption, is a representation apart from life. But as the pageant proceeds, particularly in the second half, its *Orlando*-like movement through English history begins to split open Woolf's illusionism by virtue of confusing characters in the text as readers or viewers of the pageant with our own role as readers of the text.

Miss La Trobe's initial activities include organizing the costumes and props and also hiding the gramophone that will be the thread uniting what is otherwise an insufficiently coherent performance to come (63). She reflects, as Woolf herself has, on the status of convention in what at first glance may seem to be only lament, but which is actually something quite different. Like Orlando's house, Pointz Hall is the very embodiment of a conventional unconscious. An "invisible procession" (69) of the dead streams through it as the living go about the tasks of the day. "The books in the wall . . . were pan pipes" (68); the house has its "garden, bathed in sun," beneath its windows (69). The conventional looks natural thanks to years of usage. The floor of being is, as it turns out here, not nature or essence but tradition itself. The topography of High Modernism has been turned upside down. "'I was born. In this bed,'" says Lucy Swithin (70), presumably to secure her sense of roots and of a relation to place and to ground. But "her voice died away," remarks the narrator, while Lucy murmurs, "'we live in others'" (70). As the audience begins to assemble for the pageant, its private or honest behavior already looks like part of a play, even to the people participating in it. Convention weights rather than weighs one down. The audience are "truants no more" (73), says Woolf, precisely because of convention. They are, after all, spectators at a play. Similarly, Lucy can leave a "sentence unfinished" (74) because she knows that convention will complete it. The "odds and ends" (74) out of which the audience is made up get stitched into a single group by virtue of convention. Mr. Page, the reporter, aptly named, even says that he is present "'in place of my grandfather or great-grandfather'" (75).

The point becomes clear once the pageant starts. "Then the play began," says Woolf. "Was, or was it not," she asks in the sentence following, "the play?" (76). What is representation and what is life? Where is the line between them? The question governs Woolf's handling of the pageant and the audience's response to it throughout the novel. The continuity of the pageant's illusionism is, of course, regularly called into question. When Miss La Trobe's gramophone, for example, "chuff[s]" (78), it interrupts the illusion. But because everyone knows the gramophone has a role in the illusion, its imperfections eventually become part of the illusion, too. When Albert, the village idiot, wanders into the picture, his own Wordsworthian role-playing also makes him part of the pageant: in this representation of English country life, he simply plays himself. "There was such a medley of things going on" (90), says Woolf, that one "could make nothing of it" (90). Confusion as to boundaries abounds. The line between the real and the represented becomes terribly frayed in this open-air amateur extravaganza, and it makes the audience nervous. The book's structure of representational assumption—the pageant here, life there—begins to unravel even as it is maintained. Woolf's crosswriting now structures plot itself.

The gramophone's announcement, *"Dispersed are we"* (95), is customarily read as a sign of wartime lament; it is also the reverse. There is no division at all, but instead so overdetermined a sense of both community and the bonds of convention upon which it is based that the audience's desire to make sense of the pageant ironically testifies to its strength rather than to its defects. As Giles runs to the house and back during the intermission, his own presumably natural, extra-pageant activities are, in Woolf's description, as conventionalized as those in a play, especially since skipping about the lawn reminds him not of nature and innocence but of "the rules of the game" (99), as Woolf puts it, that he played there as a child.

At the text's almost exact center, Mrs. Manresa makes the inversion plain. Dragging poor Giles about the tea party in the barn, she pulls him, says Woolf, "in and out" (107). But what, after all, is "in" and what is "out" in this sly, shrewd, and new assessment of the relation between fact and fiction? "'I wish,'" says a dazed and confused Isa, "'the play didn't run in my head'" (113). And this only at intermission, or between the acts. The difference between play and life, representation and reality, convention and freedom has now begun to unravel overtly. Even the desire in conversation for people to say "whatever came into their heads" (113) meets with a discovery of the conventional and the expected rather than with something fugitive or hidden. The natural scene "seemed," says Woolf, to call people "out of their private lives, out of their separate avocations, and made to take part" (117). Take part—as though a role in a play— in what? In a community that is already in place and that is already a pageant in its own right. No wonder old Bart finds himself "standing in front of the book case," remembering Shelley's line that "poets . . . are the legislators of mankind" (115), although failing to add—there is no need to do so in *Between the Acts*—that the legislation is customarily, to use Shelley's own word, "unacknowledged."

Once the pageant resumes, Woolf is altogether frank in breaking down the normative categories of lived experience. As the audience returns to its seats, "[v]oices chattered" (119), whether from the stage or the audience itself it is now impossible from Woolf's narration to tell. "The inner voice," she says, "the other voice was saying" (119). Is "the inner voice" the same as "the other voice"? The famous "scraps and fragments" (120) that Miss La Trobe hears are not, like T. S. Eliot's, broken off from obscured wholes; they are instead part of the increasing cacophony combining pageant proper, audience response, and the grumbling and awkward mediation between them of the spluttering gramophone. The confusion between inner and outer, spectator and representation, gets worse and worse, especially when the villagers appear in the pageant in the role of villagers (125). As awkwardness continues to mar the performance, Miss La Trobe eventually gives up, "paralyzed" (140), as though she, too, were part of a parody. Convinced that "her power had left her, had failed" (140), she has in fact succeeded in putting together and taking apart coherence itself in an unwitting theatrical version of Woolf's own crosswriting. Says Miss La Trobe to her lover, Miss Rodgers, as the confusion intensifies: "'You've stirred me in my unacted part'" (153). However unacted or unaffected, Miss La Trobe's feelings are nonetheless part of a "'part'" in a play, too, one called life itself. Miss La Trobe's fear that the pageant is failing because problems with the equipment force the audience to disperse and chatter (155) is, ironically, the very sign of its success as a device within the novel.

The "cackle" and "cacophony" (183) finally build to a climax with the splendid invention on Woolf's part of the mirrors onstage that show the audience its own reflection (184–85). This completes the book's movement, turning the opposition between audience and stage inside out in wonderfully graphic manner. The actors are "reluctant" (195) to leave, leaving the distinction between stage and a dispersing audience perilous again. Like the High Romantic "cacophony" (209) of the birds in the tree behind which Miss La Trobe has hidden, the daunting cackle of tongues as the pageant and the swirl of response to it build and build is really a celebration, a celebration of language, of what Bakhtin calls the carnivalesque. It is the kind of celebration particular in fact to the form of the novel, and which Woolf here, in the grand gesture one always expected from her last novel but was afraid to ask for, brings to as durable and influential a climax historically as does Joyce's very different one in *Finnegans Wake* (1941). Rather than lament an insurmountable difference between pageant and life, text and reality, *Between the Acts'* strategy undoes this very structure of representational assumption by taking representation itself to its extreme.

The novel's turning inside out has the effect of destabilizing the ground of sense for Woolf's readers even more than for her characters; it is also a fair literary simulation of Woolf's own apparent state of mind during the late Thirties. The price of her aesthetic breakthrough in *Between the Acts* is the deracination of everything upon which ground is customarily struck. The semiotic porousness of the pageant—its self-excessiveness, its almost self-conscious hyperbolization and mockery of the very conventions of drama it means, presumably, simply to employ—is, like the audience's need to fix it interpretatively, an allegory: an allegory for the structure of Woolf's crosswriting and the ways in which we read it.

9

the BODY ENGLISH

The British Invasion—the blitz of British rock and roll bands on American radio from 1964 to 1966—well exemplifies the dynamics of exchange that define rock and roll as a form, whether before or after the emergence of a white rock and roll supposedly distinct from an African-American one despite common roots, however revised, in the same rhythm and blues tradition. As a trope, the British Invasion is a metalepsis, rendering the late early and the early late. Those once defeated by those they once colonized could, as it were, now point to these onetime revolutionaries and condemn them as colonizers in their own right. The British Invasion represents no less than the return of the American repressed—Afro-America. The Rolling Stones' "Paint It Black" (1966) is a summary emblem for its fundamental concerns. We should remember, too, that British rock is working class in social origin and, in the case of the Mersey sound, also provincial. Here in fact dandy England bonds directly with black urbanity to cool off and rearticulate the American country cowboy, including the cowboy's rela-tion to black American culture. The paisley the British brought to the clothing styles associated with rock and roll in the Sixties is a fair metaphor for Pater's psychedelic sublime, the supplement the cowboy needed to see that the world's boundaries were fluxional fictions, ideologically constructed. Here all things mix and collide in a performance of its principles—boots and scarves, jeans and long hair; class, gender, ethnicity. Even the masculinist biases with which rock and roll must deal as a discursive convention thereby become reified practices subject to mockery and reflection.

The full importance of British rock and roll cannot be grasped unless it is seen in the context of the long historical relation between Britain and its former American colonies. Instead of playing out the normal tale of the British original and the American copy (Scott and Cooper, say), British Invasion rock and roll does the reverse: it privileges American forms as original and a once-original British culture as copy. The British blues revival of the 1960s—John Mayall, for example, and his first guitarist, Eric Clapton—decolonize the same American repressed that is exposed by the British Invasion in a wider pop vein. Like the sound of British Invasion bands such as the Kinks, the Yardbirds (the band's name alludes to Charlie Parker's nickname), and, of course, the Who, the decidedly truculent quality of these blues bands also leads to the violence characteristic of heavier and heavier British guitar playing. Jimmy Page founded Led Zeppelin in 1968 out of the ashes of the old Yardbirds (the band first toured as the New Yardbirds), like Jeff Beck and Clapton part of a group of English guitarists who loom large in a remarkably continuous and traditional rock and roll history. The Rolling Stones' Keith Richards is a key early link between American rhythm and blues and British Invasion music, largely because the power and size of his rhythm guitar almost directly translates the romp energy and riff specificity of soul studio horn sections into the tighter setting of the electric rock and roll band. Richards is the Memphis Horns, guitar style. No wonder a (fallen) American guitarist like Dickie Betts of the Allman Brothers Band could remark of heavy blues guitar, "We used our guitars like a brass section" (Wexler 1993, 256). The British blues revival also provided a climate of emergence for a host of high-quality English soul singers, including Stevie Winwood (the Spencer Davis Group, Winwood's group before the reflexively named Traffic, is also a belated rhythm and blues band), Joe Cocker, Rod Stewart (Jeff Beck's singer when Beck started his own psychedelic blues ensemble after leaving the Yardbirds in 1967), Van Morrison, and, in the Seventies, Graham Parker and Phil Collins. Cocker, for example, turns a Beatles tune like "With a Little Help from My Friends" back into the rhythm and blues song it almost was on *Sgt. Pepper* (1967). Cocker also goes on to perform and record in New York in the 1970s with many of the Atlantic r & b sessionmen of the mid-1960s, a number of whom had worked for years with King Curtis (see Meisel 1976a).

The British Invasion's most luxuriant yield was, of course, the Beatles. Beatlemania was capped by the band's back-to-back appearances on *The Ed Sullivan Show* in New York in 1964, the same year that saw the signing of the Civil Rights Act and a year that serves as a kind of watershed for a change in the politics of Anglo-American form. The Beatles made no secret of their admiration for Chuck Berry and Little Richard and asked American reporters where B. B. King was playing (the reporters had never heard of B. B. King). If we have always noticed the Beatles' relation to the tradition of the dandy despite John Lennon's rocker (read "cowboy") resistance to the group's largely mod fashionability, we notice the cowboy or, musically, the country and western dimension of the Beatles far too little. The early Beatles are as much a country and western band as they are a rhythm and blues band, largely because of Buddy Holly's almost inestimable degree of influence upon them, Paul McCartney in particular (note, too, George Harrison's guitar). On *Rubber Soul* (1965), for example, songs like "Think for Yourself," "I'm Looking Through You," and "Run for Your Life" are Tex-Mex—an Austin sound—*avant la lettre;* there's even an oompah kick in all three tunes through which you can almost hear the Dixieland tuba common to the history of country and r & b alike. This is probably why Paul plays a hollow body electric bass rather than a solid body one. He uses its powder-puff sound both to advance the history of his instrument (hollow body electric bass as a newer fillip still in the new metal environment) and, at the same time, to return the sound to its Dixieland origins.

The title of *Rubber Soul* is a useful trope with which to describe the plastic processing at work in rock and roll that transforms the presumably native into another kind of "other"'s history—the history of the oppressor. As a trope, "Rubber Soul" well represents the now genuinely electric processing at work in the psychedelic sublime; soul, or American nativity, is turned into a flexible, mass-produced element that can be reworked into any shape at all. The famous Beatle vocal harmonies, for example, are, like those of the Who or the Kinks, mannerized falsetto versions of back-up girl singers on rhythm and blues records or of the great girl groups themselves, whose whole sound gets situated within the Beatles' larger, more historically self-conscious and ambitious one. *Revolver* (1966b) puts into question any absoluteness that this rubbering may seem to produce, since even its sense as a title is open to question. "Revolver" as a trope splits its husk, playing endlessly between two senses, the gun and the turntable, each one destabilizing the other by putting the other in place by foil or negation, much as Paul's pose as dandy both clashes and commingles with John's as cowboy. Where the interpretative revolving stops with the Beatles, nobody knows.

The best proof that the British Invasion was the return of the American repressed is Jimi Hendrix, a black American from Seattle whose proper destiny was available to him only in England. Indeed, with Hendrix, both our paradigms—the African-American one and the Romantic one—overlay one another. No figure in the history of rock and roll more plainly displays the cowboy and the dandy compact both in semiotics and in music. And no figure save perhaps Miles Davis (with whom Hendrix became friends) more plainly represents black urbanity's crossings at so late a moment in blues-tradition history. Nor has any other guitarist save Chuck Berry, his anxiety of influence, had so absolute and lasting an influence upon the whole history of the medium. Once Little Richard's guitarist—and once a member of King Curtis's band (see Wexler 1993, 199)—Hendrix uses costume to enjamb cowboy and dandy and yokes them together musically by virtue of an r & b in overdrive to which the prerogatives of self-exile allowed him, like Joyce, to go. The blown-up guitar is, as we shall see throughout this last phase of our discussion, an English version—the English version— of Berry's guitar from a safe and steady distance.

The deep affinity between British rock and American rhythm and blues is plainest here, when an American original shares in the invention of the heavy electric guitar that is a trademark British contribution to the history of rock and roll, its manifest American sources notwithstanding (see Palmer 1992). In Hendrix, cowboy and dandy, black and white, English and American, electric and voice— all these familiar differences or oppositions—are trampled, reconstituted, reversed, blurred, crossed over. The voice—a weak but present voice not so much struggling as simply coexisting, languorously, with the heavy guitar—has become little more than a formal necessity, a bow to convention even as the conventionality that customarily situates it is being redrawn by the guitar itself. Hendrix's chordings, whether jumping, vibrating, or expanding, derive from Berry, although they are also jazz guitar strategies that suggest just how many prehistories of influence are at work in his sound. The extended soloing (Hendrix has to be included among the initiators of what is now yet another rock convention) is itself a jazz derivation. Conventionally, rock and roll solos, unlike jazz solos, were always short, to the point, confined to a chorus or a verse or maybe both. But like, perhaps even more than, the British blues revivalists into whose atmosphere he fell as an émigré—Beck, Clapton, and Page, for example—Hendrix also adopts for the guitar the more improvisatory jazz stance.

Are You Experienced? (1967), Hendrix's first album, shows us the familiar series of crossings out of which his achievement emerges and which his singular powers reorganize into a new rock mode altogether continuous with rock and roll tradition as a whole. Almost parodying Berry, the title tune begins with a series of scraping, hacking guitar chords that both redouble and revise Berry's habitual song openings, among other feints by squashing their customary harmonic progressions. This definitive early Hendrix juggernaut still keeps the voice crooning, sliding over the rough band behind it, but it also accents the very difference between voice and instrument that his career otherwise overcomes. As a song, in fact, "Are You Experienced?" is almost an anti-tune, the harmonically typological promise or expectation of deliverance in the chorus meaningless when we get there. What we get instead, on the third chorus in particular, is a long, characteristically Hendrix solo. Chordings are often set aside completely in favor of the single-note noodling common to the British scene into which he had walked, although this is also another feint, since the single-notedness is pressured, even discredited, in its oscillation with power chords that are themselves usually unconcerned with progression. Here Hendrix challenges the funky duo behind him (a power trio, Hendrix's English band included Noel Redding on bass and Mitch Mitchell on drums) to see how well it can maintain the backbeat while he trashes almost every category upon which his performance ironically depends, including at times the groove itself.

"Purple Haze" is really a slow funk tune. The guitar riffs that define the song perhaps even more than its vocals are horn-section chordings like Berry's, while the unison bass and guitar between statements of the melody momentarily bring the soul side of the sound forward. Hendrix also counterposes the calculating cool of his voice to the heat of the guitar. As his brief career progresses, however, he almost loses interest in singing, which becomes an ambiguous protocol. He grows more and more preoccupied with the ax alone, which needs the voice for the sake of contrast. His guitar can, of course, only emerge against his voice, each muddying the boundaries the other has drawn. "Voodoo Chile" also shows just how much Hendrix superadds hard urban blues soloing to the rhythmic fluidity of the Memphis Berry, crossing these cousin styles with an intimacy legal only in the environment of exile.

Subsequent recordings by Hendrix's British band include even fuller elaborations of our paradigm. "Third Stone from the Sun" on *Axis: Bold as Love* (1968a) is rhythmically a swing tune ("Bold as Love" is similar), featuring Redding's walking bass and Mitchell's wonderfully easy drums, which include ride cymbals worthy of proper jazz drumming. Here Hendrix's chordings on the verse are almost conventional jazz guitar—Wes Montgomery peering over a precipice he had never imagined was there—while the bridge is a kind of mock-soul series of heavier chordings that sound like studio horns. But the bridge is so brief that one hardly notices it before a rather superfluous vocal emerges for one chorus following the official guitar solo to remind us again of the number of crossings at work in the sound's structures and sequences alike.

Not only, then, does Hendrix loot the past; he also prophesies the future in numerous ways. The extraordinary "Gypsy Eyes" on *Electric Ladyland* (1968b), for example, combines voice and guitar in harmony at tune's start in a sardonic premonition of the pop phase of George Benson's career; it also presages hard-funk drive guitar of the kind common to rock-and-soul groups like the B. T. Express. "Have You Ever Been (to Electric Ladyland)" is a surprisingly light, almost Bensonesque tune in retrospect, although Hendrix's own overtracked back-up vocals sound like Memphis girls singing behind him. (Is there a hint of soul tradition, too, in this splitting of one's own voice?) Indeed, "Dolly Dagger" is at times a proto-Philly disco tune, with decided funk chords, but played in light Montgomery mode.

The historical density of Hendrix's achievement is clear in a fresh way at the end of his career with his last group, the Band of Gypsys, composed of Buddy Miles on drums and Billy Cox on bass. A slower and more plainly rhythm and blues band than the earlier British one, the Band of Gypsys is still so original that even its return to roots sounds like Hendrix rather than the roots. To be sure, the guitar solos are franker, single-note jazzish ones, at least in the first half of choruses, but the single-note jazz lines turn as a rule into hyper-Berry/Django Reinhardt chordings in the second four or eight bars of a given solo chorus. "Power of Soul" on the Band of Gypsys' only album, *Band of Gypsys* (1970), is Hendrix's overt announcement of these changes. A Buddy Miles composition, the tune begins with virtuosic Montgomery-like jazz guitar before it turns back (or ahead) to characteristic Hendrix. It is as though he gives us a taste of his scholarship before charging forward on his own, this kind of self-revision the very logic of a given tune's musical narrative. Hendrix's rhythm and blues roots become altogether clear on two other Buddy Miles tunes on *Band of Gypsys,* "Changes" and "We Gotta Live Together," a light soul chopper and a stomping funk groove respectively. Buddy Miles went on to form the Buddy Miles Express after Hendrix's death in 1970, one among a few but telling examples of r & b musicians crossing over into heavy rock this early, and the beginning of a harder r & b tradition that has natural ancestors in James Brown and progeny in punk and hip hop alike.

BOB DYLAN, OF COURSE, is a manifest crossing of cowboy and dandy, although he is also, like Armstrong or Muddy Waters, a crossing of the customary relation between voice and instrument that locates his achievement within the history of blues tradition as well. Dylan's Romantic overdeterminations are palpable and overt, not only in his self-naming but also in his lyrics and mythographies. *John Wesley Harding* (1968), for example, an album named for a gun-slinger, includes "All Along the Watchtower," a song lyrically derived from the tradition of English Romanticism at work, say, in Browning's "Childe Roland to the Dark Tower Came" (Hendrix covered the tune on *Electric Ladyland*). Dylan's musicality, however, is as a rule more compelling than his Romanticism, and it places him at the center of rock and roll history even more powerfully and directly than his Romanticism does. It is the move from acoustic to electric, from the solitary folk setting to the rock and roll band, that is the decisive moment in Dylan's itinerary, and it is so superb an example of our paradigm that its importance to our story cannot be overestimated.

The moment comes with the first side of *Bringing It All Back Home* in 1965 (1965a), and its electric inventiveness is the signature of Dylan's central preoccupations throughout his career. It revises the primacy of Dylan's voice by making it an instrument rather than a natural curiosity in relation to the band now behind it. Speech or voice in singing is never really either one, since voice is an instrument from the start when it sings (hence Dylan's harmonica is the perpetual suspension of these oppositions, like accordion a combination of air and machine). The second thing to note about *Bringing It All Back Home*, however, is that the second side is once again acoustic. It is as though the crossing to the city, to the electric from the primary, has been reversed. The electric is thrown into shocking, retroactive relief. But, of course, the pattern of reversal is, as it turns out, not unfamiliar, in either Dylan's earlier work or his later.

Like the phrase "bringing it all back home," Dylan's language is structured throughout his career by tropes of return. The title of *Highway 61 Revisited* (1965b), for example, recalls a central thread in our own story, and in much the same way. Highway 61 connects New Orleans with Chicago and parallels the Mississippi. To revisit it is to see the relation between country and city in all its mutuality. I have already, in the introduction, called attention to this structure in the lyrics to "I Shall Be Released," which served as a paradigm for the unexpected movement "from the West back to the East" that a critical late Romanticism like Dylan's or Oscar Wilde's imports to the hoot and holler of colonial Romanticism, whether English or American. *Highway 61 Revisited* situates country and city in relation to one another, much as the passage "from the West back to the East" reverses cowboy and dandy, bringing the cowboy back to his enablement in prior sources or frontiers that he is obliged to cross or violate as the price required for respecting their visionary authority. Indeed, "I Shall Be Released," which was first recorded by the Band on *Music from Big Pink* in 1968, was not recorded by Dylan himself until *Self-Portrait* in 1970. The mild irony—the author's belated emergence *in propria persona*, as it were—is characteristic of the recursive irony that informs Dylan's work as a whole. What was shocking about Dylan when he appeared as a youngster on the folk scene in the early 1960s was that his voice sounded like an old man's, already scraped and tiered with usage, residue, influence. Even the last fully acoustic album, Dylan's fourth recording, is provocatively entitled (as we can see now) *Another Side of Bob Dylan* (1964) and already has our familiar structure on full display. The lyrics to "My Back Pages" give us our paradigm in a readily temporal form: "I was so much older then," sings a retrospective Dylan, "I'm younger than that now." The paradox is both logical and familiar. The retrospect of belatedness is what ironically produces the refreshments of enhanced perception. Earlier and later define one another in the unstable play between them that makes up our sense of the present.

Bringing It All Back Home itself is a play on our paradigm in any number of ways, from its title trope to its lyrics. "Bringing it *all* back home"—"all"—is presumably the singer's, or at least the singing's, achievement, without any loss involved. But it is only the returning that is full, not the home that receives it (*"bringing* it all back home"), which is, apparently, lacking enough to require it. Where is an inflection to guide us in accenting the figure? There is not even a pronoun assigned to the participle "bringing"; agency in the song is the function of an unnamable dynamic that connects by virtue of separation and leaves subjects at the mercy of objects— home and exile, then and now, New Orleans and Chicago, Zimmerman and Dylan.

"Love Minus Zero," the album's most bewitching tune melodically, is also its most poetic, and describes these mechanisms with often astonishing exactitude. The overlay of colloquialisms one upon another ("Draw conclusions on the wall") shows how the meaning of a word or the movement of a mood is governed by frame. The song substitutes a transitive version of an intransitive verb to tilt cliché into feeling ("The young, they speak of the future; / My love, she speaks softly"). Nor do opposites simply attract in Dylan's world: "She knows there's no success like failure, / And that failure's no success at all." Success and failure do indeed define one another by virtue of their difference, but that doesn't mean they're simply the same, mere opposite sides of one coin. Like pleasure and pain, loss and gain, country and city, or East and West, success and failure, too, are calibrations within any number of signifying fields.

(The title of *Blonde on Blonde* [1966] formulates in a visual key the notion of differential sense posed here: how can one establish boundaries, margins, outlines when the terms of a given discourse are apparently homogeneous? How can Bob Zimmerman, for example, find a place in signifying fields whose only distinguishing principle is blonde on blonde?) We see the same principle at work at tune's end: "My love, she's like some raven / At my window with a broken wing." It is not clear until the last word of the line what modifying—indeed, what substantive—position each term in the sentence has in relation to the others. Will "broken" modify "window," as we might be led to suspect, momentarily, leading us to await "pane" at the end of the line instead of "wing"? Even Dylan's semantic coherence obeys the logic of deferred action, much as his visionary Romanticism came to triumph early on over his folk realism.

THE LINE IN THE sand drawn by Dylan in the move from acoustic to electric has an equivalent in Led Zeppelin's heavy-metal inventiveness in 1968, another major moment in our history and an excellent example of the kind of structural link behind otherwise unrelated dimensions of the Sixties like the folk scene and English rock. Zep's is a fiercely revisionary project compared, for example, to either the world-historical calm of the Beatles or even the Stones. If the big band in jazz diminished with the small-group modernism of Parker, it died a second death in rock and roll with the emergence of heavy metal in England. The logic is already implicit in Chuck Berry, but a commerce with rocking saxophone culture remains in Berry's sound—and in the Beatles' and the Stones' as well—despite the foregrounded guitar. With Zep, however, all this changes irrevocably, although on Berry's shoulders. What is missing in Zep without our noticing it? The horns. That role has now been replaced, thanks to Jimmy Page, with pure electric; the rhythmic wall once provided by the horn section in a swing or, later on, in a rhythm and blues band is now in the hands of a single, thundering electric guitarist. The Who's term "maximum r & b" well describes this characteristic achievement of British rock as a whole. Before Page formed Zep in 1968, Jerry Wexler had actually wanted to market Page, an astonishingly busy sessionman in the early 1960s, as a rhythm and blues guitarist (Wexler 1993, 158, 222). Like the head riffs of Cream tunes, the opening riff of Zep's "Whole Lotta Love" (1969), for example, sounds like a horn head. (When the riff does indeed get translated back into rhythm and blues horns, as it does on King Curtis's cover of "Whole Lotta Love" (1971), the difference is nonetheless palpably stiff, although the fact of the choice on Curtis's part is itself provocative.) Catch the saxophone logic of Page's rhythm guitar—his metal riffmaking, after all, is really a trash play on the stutter of soul horn arrangements and the drones of Phil Spector's walls of sound. It is also a revisionary ratio. Page succeeds in retroactively structuring a new distinction into the very flow, as he now recreates it, of rock and roll history: the distinction between horn music and guitar music, rendering outmoded the very locus of his own anxiety as a function of extending its logic.

What is excised in Zep is precisely the originary modality of rock and roll enablement—the saxophone—transumed into the higher electric key of the guitar. Like the Who, Zep establishes an irrevocable boundary in musical history: before and after serious electric. This is the Shelleyan or Paterian project whose stability comes, ironically, from its "perpetual weaving and unweaving" of rock and roll's modalities—the psychedelic sublime in overdrive—and which rocks the thundering materiality of electric rock at the moment it rolls it into place. Zep's modality is a kind of hyperbolic minimalism or transistorization—its version of Paterian *ascesis*—not unlike the kind represented by the trap set's invention, which transistorizes marching band percussion. With Zep, the disposition of forms is compensatory: heavy guitar is a field of power bred to rival a burdensome acoustic tradition of rocking horns subdued at the very moment it is honored (the title of the band's 1976 album *Presence* is an effective irony, since Zep actually privileges metal over horns, collapsing the breath or presence that blows reeds). Zep's gesture is a landmark moment in the history of music whether you like them or not; they up the ante, electrify rock and roll full scale, and so change our perception, as the saying goes, not only of music history but of music as such. Zep's psychedelic sublime restructures our very notion of music as one depending first and foremost on the difference between electric and acoustic. The improper play of proper names between singer and guitarist is also an instance of our paradigm: Page is text or culture, Plant nature; and yet, as alloys one of the other—as a loop or crossing—the nature/culture op-position that they represent gets undone by virtue of being put in place.

Metal and punk are, as we can see, then, from Zep, continuous with rhythm and blues, too. In fact, the technical continuity be-tween r & b and heavy metal arguably leads directly to punk itself, a relation no more clearly displayed in punk's recording history than on the Ramones' odd and symptomatic album, *End of the Century* (1980), produced, uncannily enough, by Phil Spector. It retrospec-tively allows us to see our history with extraordinary vividness. It collides two rock and roll visions so in accord with each other that their overlapping leads to a stark discovery of their differences, a discovery that clarifies the historical relation between Spector and the Ramones and that rediscovers and rearticulates our paradigm all over again. Spector interprets the Ramones as a profoundly tradi-tional band by nestling the guitar-machine quartet at the center of his legendary "wall of sound." Suddenly, the stuttering rock and roll guitar turbine familiar in metal and punk alike doesn't stand alone in its humorous/heroic way but occupies the hub of a sound that it has always implied but never really spelled out: rhythm and blues horns and their relation to later guitar.

What is proverbially impressive about Spector's production style, however, is also what turns out to be the trouble with it on *End of the Century*. The Ramones are famous for subtraction, not for ex-humation of their sources. The effect is to undo by use of Spector's horns and strings—however slightly, and with real though ironic re-wards—the Ramones' own hard-won economy. Few rock bands have packed so much history into so few gestures, and the history they pack includes Spector's "wall of sound." On *End of the Century*, we hear it on top of its later transistorization. Here Spector's is an older technology confronting a more evolved one. The Ramones, after all, don't just inherit Spector directly; they also inherit him via his (silent) presence in big-metal rock. Droning, thwacking Zep and Who guitars are already a transistorization, a microminiaturization, a "chip" of Spector's (largely) acoustic, naturally produced wall of sound, dominated very largely by horns even in the old days. Horns, of course, are simply redundant when it comes to bands like Zep and the Ramones alike. The Ramones have already transistorized the transistors and so stand at two removes from Spector himself,

who forces them to unpack, to undress—to decompress their influences and stand with old relations for a family picture of the kind
we don't ordinarily get to see.

The cover of Spector's old Ronettes hit "Baby I Love You" (1963)
is the album's most dramatic departure from the usual Ramones aus-
terity, yet it is also the song on which Spector and the Ramones nevertheless meet at a point most natural to them both. The blasts of
staccato strings blunt the edge of Joey's supermannered singing by
outmannering it, but they also situate his voice in the early Sixties
context from which his hiccupy style emerges. This may be to call
his bluff, although he's still a decent enough crooner to answer the
rhythm and blues drill. The result: a classic Ramones paradox of art-
ful sincerity, mannered honesty, and committed nihilism despite—
perhaps now because of—the superadded Spector production. The
double entendre in the title hook of "I'm Affected" explores these
paradoxes—these rhetorical loops and musical crossings—and, in
the process, the central paradox of rock and roll itself. What is moving, what is loaded with "affect" or emotion, is also that which is
"affected" or put on. The natural emerges from a relation to culture.
Joey's yodel-plunge vibrato characteristically exchanges and identifies affect and affectation, matter and manner, nature and culture,
cowboy and dandy. The band's phony-family bit is another instance
of the blood/fiction paradox. For the Ramones, rock and roll is a self-
conscious discourse of affectations that moves us despite—or perhaps because of—itself.

Hip hop produces a new rhythm and blues climate that is also
structurally traditional and that returns us to our paradigm once
again, even before the mode softens and uncovers its relation to historical materials, among them the relation of horns and electric. Hip
hop rearranges the relation between voice and band that we see in
Armstrong or Dylan, although with the greater complexity that later
moments in history make inevitable. Rapping promotes the speak-
erly purity of voice and the difference of voice from rhythm, even as
it collapses the two into one another and collapses the difference between instrument and machine in the band itself in endlessly cali-
brated ways. On the one hand, it treats voice like a voice, a speaking
voice. Rhyme, meanwhile, fosters the illusion of an easy, echoic link
between words and things by making the relation look more natural
than it is. On the other hand, of course, rapping makes voice more

percussive and less lyrical than ever; voice is no longer lyrical, even melodic at all. Its sheer manneredness undoes the chattiness it presumably represents. The rapper's absolute and personal presence is the careful function of a field of usages, some native to the body, some not. Recent legal questions regarding the status of originality in hip hop uses of sampling and the status of the proper in hip hop uses of obscenity have actually served to clarify what is simply its dialectical presentation of the boundaries that situate any number of familiar differences, chief among them influence and originality, ownership and servitude, clean and dirty, and, of course, black and white. Hip hop's preoccupations are familiar and recall the crossings that structure rock tradition as a whole.

a CODA on CANONICITY and MYTHOLOGY

A mong the questions my praxis may have raised is that of the presumable inevitability of a canon as a functional principle in a tradition, in rock and roll, for example, or in literature. My arguments, whether musical or literary, have as a rule required canonical texts among the beads, to use Emerson's figure, that I need to string together a critical story. Like young athletes imitating stars, musicians and writers, however unconsciously, require precursors, too, simply to have a sense of what they're up to. Michael Jordan imitates, then overcomes Julius Erving, much as the Ramones copy, then throttle heavy metal bands, or Shakespeare swerves from, then transumes Marlowe.

What, then, is canonicity? Given Pater's—and rock's—psychedelic sublime, the notion of a canon as a stable Arnoldean lode of absolute value is, of course, not what I have in mind. What is a canon, then, functionally? The structure of influence displayed by canons is, simply put, a discursive necessity. Made by poets, musicians, and ballplayers themselves, canons are internal, functional inevitabilities, not external impositions. Canonical figures allow latecomers to know how to do something in the first place, whether writing poetry, playing a horn, or playing basketball. They make traditions work; they allow individual expression to occur. Influence is ironically necessary for one to become oneself.

Hence my insistence on canonicity is designed not to maintain an orthodoxy in the present or in the future, but to do just the reverse—to maintain a ground against which the possibility of future originality can be measured, heard, felt, written, played. It is without a canon, ironically, that one is doomed to repeat the past. Because *langue* and *parole*, to use Saussure's model, are mutual—each needs the other for its sustenance—an overt, functional canonicity is always in place in any signifying system. Any articulation in any kind of language is a riff on a collective and inherited paradigm. If you don't know it, you can't hear or speak. Authority is a structural condition, not a personal problem. Oedipal formations and other apostrophes, whether political or aesthetic, are the means by which paradigms are personified for subjects and objects alike, the way historical forces enter human activity, and the way human activity has a relation to historical process.

Nor should we forget that temporality is the condition in which the play of canonicity and belatedness, influence and originality, mythology and experience occurs. "Every writer *creates* his own precursors," writes Borges in his essay on Kafka; his or her work "modifies our conception of the past, as it will modify the future" (1951, 201). History is made from later achievements that restructure our sense of earlier ones. Woolf's *Orlando,* for example, becomes canonical only after magic realism becomes widespread as a fictional practice; then, retroactively, *Orlando* becomes a model for the form, since it turns out to have organized it paradigmatically. Similarly, by requiring horn culture by its negation, Led Zep produces a precursor in rhythm and blues at the very moment that the precursor is vanquished.

If art is the interrogation of hegemonic ideologies, then canonicity in rock, as in literature, is also the power to organize the historical overdeterminations out of which hegemony is made as a rival and repressive mode of reading the past. It is an "opportunity," to use Pater's words, that comes, ironically, from a "restriction" (1889, 107). Because of their semiotic porousness, texts always exceed themselves, thereby opening their signifying fields against the closure that given interpretative communities require in order to shut down questions, play, exchange, multiculturalism. Hence the distinction between the efficiency of aesthetic procedure and the care-laden sluggishness of ideological reflex.

What, then, is the relation of canonicity to mythology and of mythology to experience? Like hegemony, although on the receiving end, mythologies, too, are misreadings, reductions, literalizations of canonical texts. "What the poets said in rhyme," writes Woolf, "the young translated into practice" (1928a, 27). "All experience is art," writes a Wildean Ishmael Reed in *Yellow Back Radio Broke-Down* (1969,75). Or, as Wilde himself describes the process in "The Decay of Lying":

> Life imitates art far more than Art imitates Life. We have all seen in our own day in England how a certain curious and fascinating type of beauty, invented and emphasized by two imaginative painters, has so influenced life that whenever one goes to a private view or to an artistic salon one sees, here the mystic eyes of Rossetti's dream, the long ivory throat, the strange square-cut jaw, the loosened shadowy hair that he so ardently loved, there the sweet maidenhood of "The Golden Stair," the blossom-like mouth and weary loveliness of the "Laus Amoris," the passion-pale face of Andromeda, the thin hands and lithe beauty of the Vivien in "Merlin's Dream." And it has always been so. A great artist invents a type, and Life tries to copy it, to re-produce it in a popular form, like an enterprising publisher. (1891, 307)

Mythology in practice is myth—a belief in the unitary interpretative regimes that ideology fixes in the porousness of given signifying fields. Mythologies are the interpretative residue of canonical practices such as Shelley's, Emerson's, Pater's, or Zep's, the reduced or degraded yield of aesthetic discourses prepared for experiential consumption. Of course, what forces we think do the cooking—Marxist, Freudian, and Foucauldian are as a rule the likeliest in our own age—are the functions of interpretative choices, too, choices presumably determined in turn by the forces that they try to represent. Hence crossing over is also the structure of cause and effect in historiography. Crossing over is actually identical with the movement of overdetermination itself; its loop describes the same constitutive relation to alterity that history and historian share.

American discourse is by definition fugitive and agonistic; otherness is the perpetual and ironic condition of its originality. To be an American means that you need an antagonist, a discursive partner with whom you can argue for the benefit of your enlightenment next to his or her monarchic pallor. Every American discourse, whether colonial or slave narrative, posits—feels—a semiotic rival against whom everything is said, done, organized, personified. This overt and enabling dialogism also underwrites the one aspect of decency that American culture has at its philosophical foundation: because its discourse is comparative, it is always artificial. America's single and singular virtue is that its ground is invented, based not upon a myth of natural right or of ethnicity as ground, the kind of foundation that one finds in European history or in world history at large, but upon groundlessness as such. Artificial is good—the only good—because it means that no one can make a claim of any kind on the basis of natural categories. No culture was ever more plainly baseless than American culture is, and that is its only moral advantage over the past, including its own. The later self-correction by means of which constitutional interpretation is by definition structured institutionally insures the perpetual advantage of the latecomer over the pioneer. American culture presumes nothing, accepting, in Ivan Karamazov's words, that "everything is possible."

What, as I asked in the introduction, is the yield of these harsh ironies? The synthetic quality of America, its defining elasticity. Artificial or synthetic America—rubber-soul America in all its revolving senses—has as its real philosophical justification the fact that it has no one stable one. Crossover is the enabling precondition and active modality of American life. It is not just a hidden discursive mechanism. It is in your face. Among the jests of the Age of Exploration is that the world got severed by virtue of getting connected. People cannot be at odds without being in touch. The vivid common culture that all Americans possess is the yield of the decidedly artificial polity that America has always been even if it did not begin to know it before 1950. Cosmopolitanism was the European word for it in the nineteenth century; internationalism was Trotsky's word for it; assimilation is the old American word for it—a savingly artificial common culture. Rock and roll is the cosmopolitan culture of the second half of the twentieth century and of the century to come. The connection between politics and aesthetics is particularly obvious here, where presumably political questions turn into aesthetic ones and vice versa. America is a politics of form, a form of politics.

Like the novel in the nineteenth century, rock and roll has become a protocol of life in the late twentieth, both as pop myth and as a kind of newly canonical music taken for granted as world culture's dominant one. The modality of its study, moreover, is actually very familiar and testifies with some irony to its increasingly conservative stability as an emergent cultural norm. The study of popular culture has long dominated the very core, as the saying goes, of university curricula ever since vernacular literature departments were established in the wake of the Franco-Prussian war of 1870. If in the twentieth century we studied the entertainment of the nineteenth—novels by Thackeray or Dickens or Hardy—then in the twenty-first we will study the entertainment of the twentieth—rock and roll, film, and television. And just as vernacular literature departments adopted the methods and categories of classical and biblical scholarship and applied them to popular texts, so the study of pop culture today has adopted the methods and categories of literary criticism.

Psychedelia is the best epistemological model there is for the kind of multicultural politics and poetics that we have begun to practice in the United States as a culture trying to live up to its own ideal notion of itself—a politics of psychedelia, not a politics of experience that psychedelia both situates and overturns. Reveling in the presumable naturalness of ethnicity and its self-expression is not, of course, the answer to anything. One has to be careful that, in rejecting the tyranny of one culture over another, one does not also reject assimilation, the possibility—the clear and present reality—of a hybrid, shared culture assembled by any series of once-marginalized groups. Trotsky was killed for his internationalism by the nationalist Stalin, and the Soviet Union was eventually dismembered by the free expression of ethnic nationalities. With equal blindness, American conservatism misrepresents the common culture of the United States as the reflection of a fixed and eternal sphere of value, not as a consensual and historical invention. Then again, separatist multiculturalism—a nice oxymoron—does the same from an equivalent base in superannuated blood categories. When Americans grow infatuated with religions of nature such as ethnicity or fixed value, they are asking for trouble. The myths of ethnicity and fixity are among Europe's chief inventions of the nineteenth century. They led not only to the formation of the great nations of Germany and Italy but also to the racial logic of Auschwitz. Americans are federalist, not naturalist, but this self-knowledge is too often only implicit and needs teasing out so as to rescue us from the tacky and dangerous games of Left and Right alike. To such noxious and sloppy self-representations, we should be able to respond more adequately than our traditional political and formal vocabularies allow. Rock and roll provides a place to go instead, a place where roots are out of fashion after all, a place where one finds oneself because of uprootedness, not despite it. This is not a natural place, but it is a fertile one.

WORKS CITED

Bibliography

Allmendinger, Blake. 1992. *The Cowboy: Representations of Labor in an American Work Culture*. New York: Oxford University Press.

Anderson, Quentin. 1971. *The Imperial Self: An Essay in American Literary and Cultural History*. New York: Knopf.

Baker, Houston A., Jr. 1984. *Blues, Ideology, and Afro-American Literature: A Vernacular Theory*. Chicago: University of Chicago Press.

————. 1993. *Black Studies, Rap, and the Academy*. Chicago: University of Chicago Press.

Barlow, William. 1989. *"Looking Up at Down": The Emergence of Blues Culture*. Philadelphia: Temple University Press.

Barlow, William, and Cheryl Finley. 1994. *From Swing to Soul: An Illustrated History of African American Popular Music from 1930 to 1960*. Washington, D.C.: Elliott & Clark.

Barr, Marleen S. 1992. *Feminist Fabulation: Space/Postmodern Fiction*. Iowa City: University of Iowa Press.

Baudelaire, Charles. 1857. *Les Fleurs du mal*. Reprint, Paris: Garnier Frères, 1961.

————. 1859–60. "The Painter of Modern Life." Reprinted in *"The Painter of Modern Life" and Other Essays*. Translated and edited by Jonathan Mayne. London: Phaidon Press, 1964.

Benjamin, Walter. 1939. "On Some Motifs in Baudelaire." Reprinted in *Illuminations*. Edited by Hannah Arendt. Translated by Harry Zohn. New York: Schocken, 1968.

————. 1955. "Paris, Capital of the Nineteenth Century." Reprinted in *Reflections*. Edited by Peter Demetz. Translated by Edmund Jephcott. New York: Harcourt Brace Jovanovich, 1978.

Bercovitch, Sacvan. 1978. *The American Jeremiad*. Madison: University of Wisconsin Press.

Berry, Chuck. 1987. *Chuck Berry: The Autobiography*. New York: Harmony Books.

Bhabha, Homi. 1994. *The Location of Culture*. London: Routledge.

Bloom, Harold. 1992. *The American Religion: The Emergence of the Post-Christian Nation*. New York: Simon and Schuster.

———. 1994. *The Western Canon: The Books and School of the Ages*. New York: Harcourt Brace & Co.

Borges, Jorge Luis. 1951. "Kafka and His Precursors." Reprinted in *Labyrinths: Selected Stories and Other Writings*. New York: New Directions, 1964.

Bucco, Martin. 1984. *Western American Literary Criticism*. Boise: Boise State University Press.

Burke, Kenneth. 1938. "Musicality in Verse." Reprinted in *The Philosophy of Literary Form: Studies in Symbolic Action*. Third ed. 1973. Berkeley: University of California Press.

Carby, Hazel. 1994. "The Politics of Fiction, Anthropology, and the Folk: Zora Neale Hurston." In *History & Memory in African-American Culture*. Edited by Geneviève Fabre and Robert O'Meally. New York: Oxford University Press.

Carr, Ian. 1982. *Miles Davis: A Biography*. New York: Morrow.

Cather, Willa. 1912. *Alexander's Bridge*. Reprint, Lincoln: University of Nebraska Press, 1977.

———. 1913. *O Pioneers!* Reprint, New York: Penguin, 1989.

———. 1915. *The Song of the Lark*. Reprint, New York: Penguin, 1991.

———. 1918. *My Ántonia*. Reprint, Boston: Houghton Mifflin, 1988.

———. 1922a. "The Novel Démeublé." Reprinted in *Not Under Forty*. New York: Knopf, 1936.

———. 1922b. Preface to *Alexander's Bridge*. (1912). Reprint, Boston: Houghton Mifflin, 1922.

———. 1923. *A Lost Lady*. Reprint, New York: Vintage, 1990.

———. 1925. *The Professor's House*. Reprint, New York: Vintage, 1973.

———. 1926. *My Mortal Enemy*. Reprint, New York: Vintage, 1990.

———. 1927. *Death Comes for the Archbishop*. Reprint, New York: Vintage, 1990.

———. 1935. *Lucy Gayheart*. Reprint, New York: Vintage, 1976.

Cavell, Stanley. 1988. *In Quest of the Ordinary: Lines of Skepticism and Romanticism*. Chicago: University of Chicago Press.

———. 1989. *This New Yet Unapproachable America: Lectures after Emerson after Wittgenstein*. Albuquerque: Living Batch Press.

———. 1990. *Conditions Handsome and Unhandsome: The Constitution of Emersonian Perfection*. Chicago: University of Chicago Press.

Cawelti, John G. 1970. *The Six-Gun Mystique*. Second ed. 1984. Bowling Green: Bowling Green State University Popular Press.

Chambers, Jack. 1983. *Milestones 1: The Music and Times of Miles Davis to 1960*. Toronto: University of Toronto Press.

Charters, Samuel B. 1959. *The Country Blues*. New York: Rinehart & Co.

———. 1981. *The Roots of the Blues: An African Search*. Boston: Marion Boyers.

Christgau, Robert. 1972. "Chuck Berry: Eternal Rock and Roller." Reprinted in *Any Old Way You Choose It: Rock and Other Pop Music, 1967–1973*. Baltimore: Penguin, 1973.

———. 1992. "Al Green." In *The Rolling Stone Illustrated History of Rock & Roll*. New ed. Edited by Anthony DeCurtis and James Henke. New York: Straight Arrow.

Cody, William F. 1879. *The Life of Hon. William F. Cody, Known as Buffalo Bill, the Famous Hunter, Scout, and Guide: An Autobiography*. Reprint, Lincoln: University of Nebraska Press, 1978.

Cole, Bill. 1974. *Miles Davis: A Musical Biography*. New York: Morrow.

Collier, James Lincoln. 1983. *Louis Armstrong: An American Genius*. New York: Oxford University Press.

Crouch, Stanley. 1983. "Body and Soul." Reprinted in *Notes of a Hanging Judge: Essays and Reviews, 1979–89*. New York: Oxford University Press, 1990.

Curtis, William J. R. 1982. *Modern Architecture Since 1900*. Third ed. 1996. London: Phaidon.

Davis, David Brion. 1954. "Ten-Gallon Hero." Reprinted in *The American Experience: Approaches to the Study of the United States*. Edited by Hennig Cohen. Boston: Houghton Mifflin, 1968.

Davis, Dernoral. 1991. "Toward A Socio-Historical and Demographic Portrait of Twentieth-Century African-Americans." In *Black Exodus: The Great Migration from the American South*. Edited by Alferdteen Harrison. Jackson: University Press of Mississippi.

Davis, Miles, with Quincey Troupe. 1989. *Miles: The Autobiography*. New York: Simon and Schuster. Reprint, New York: Touchstone, 1990.

Defaa, Chip. 1989. *Swing Legacy*. Metuchen, N.J.: Scarecrow Press and the Institute of Jazz Studies, Rutgers University.

Dickstein, Morris. 1977. *Gates of Eden: American Culture in the Sixties*. New York: Basic Books.

Dixon, Melvin. 1994. "The Black Writer's Use of Memory." In *History & Memory in African-American Culture*. Edited by Geneviève Fabre and Robert O'Meally. New York: Oxford University Press.

Douglas, Ann. 1977. *The Feminization of American Culture*. New York: Knopf. Reprint, New York: Avon, 1978.

————. 1995. *Terrible Honesty: Mongrel Manhattan in the 1920s*. New York: Farrar, Straus and Giroux.

Douglass, Frederick. 1845. *Narrative of the Life of Frederick Douglass, an American Slave, Written by Himself.* Edited by Houston A. Baker, Jr. Reprint, New York: Viking, 1982.

Doyle, Arthur Conan. 1892a. "A Scandal in Bohemia." In *The Adventures of Sherlock Holmes.* All references are from *The Complete Sherlock Holmes.* Garden City: Doubleday, n.d.

————. 1892b. "The Copper Beeches." In *The Adventures of Sherlock Holmes.*

————. 1894. "The Musgrave Ritual." In *The Memoirs of Sherlock Holmes.*

Drake, St. Clair, and Horace R. Cayton. 1945. *Black Metropolis: A Study of Negro Life in a Northern City.* Vol. 1. Reprint and expanded ed. 1962. New York: Harper & Row.

Du Bois, W. E. B. 1903. *The Souls of Black Folk.* Reprint, New York: Penguin, 1996.

Ellison, Ralph. 1958. "The Charlie Christian Story." Reprinted in *Shadow and Act* (1964). New York: Random House. Reprint, New York: Vintage, 1972.

Ellmann, Richard. 1988. *Oscar Wilde.* New York: Knopf.

Emerson, Ken. 1995. *Doo-Dah! Stephen Foster and the Rise of American Popular Culture.* New York: Simon & Schuster.

Emerson, Ralph Waldo. 1836. *Nature.* All references are from *Selections from Ralph Waldo Emerson.* Edited by Stephen E. Whicher. New York: Houghton Mifflin, 1960.

————. 1837. *The American Scholar.*

————. 1841. "Circles." In *Essays, First Series.*

————. 1844. "The Poet." In *Essays, Second Series.*

————. 1844. "Experience." In *Essays, Second Series.*

Fabre, Geneviève, and Robert O'Meally, eds. 1994. *History & Memory in African-American Culture.* New York: Oxford University Press.

Fairbanks, Carol. 1986. *Prairie Women: Images in American and Canadian Fiction.* New Haven: Yale University Press.

Fanon, Frantz. 1952. *Black Skin, White Masks.* Translated by Charles Lam Markmann. New York: Grove Press, 1967.

Feldman, Jessica R. 1993. *Gender on the Divide: The Dandy in Modernist Literature.* Ithaca: Cornell University Press.

Felski, Rita. 1991. "The Counterdiscourse of the Feminine in Three Texts by Wilde, Huysmans, and Sacher-Masoch." *PMLA* 106:5 (Oct.), 1094–1105.

Fender, Stephen. 1981. *Plotting the Golden West: American Literature and the Rhetoric of the California Trail.* Cambridge: Cambridge University Press.

Fish, Stanley. 1989. *Doing What Comes Naturally: Change, Rhetoric, and the*

Practice of Theory in Literary and Legal Studies. Durham: Duke University Press.

Foucault, Michel. 1969. "What Is an Author?" Reprinted in *Language, Counter-Memory, Practice: Selected Essays and Interviews.* Edited by Donald F. Bouchard. Ithaca: Cornell University Press, 1977.

Frémont, John Charles. 1843. Report in *The Expedition of John Charles Frémont. Volume 1: Travels from 1838 to 1844.* Edited by Donald Jackson and Mary Lee Spence. Urbana: University of Illinois Press, 1970.

Freud, Sigmund. 1918. "From the History of an Infantile Neurosis." *The Standard Edition of the Complete Psychological Works of Sigmund Freud.* Edited by James Strachey. London: Hogarth Press and the Institute of Psycho-Analysis.

Fussell, Edwin. 1965. *Frontier: American Literature and the American West.* Princeton: Princeton University Press.

Gates, Henry Louis, Jr. 1978. "Binary Opposition in Chapter One of *The Life of Frederick Douglass.*" In *Afro-American Literature: The Reconstruction of Instruction.* Edited by Robert B. Stepto and Dexter Fisher. New York: Modern Language Association.

―――. 1988. *The Signifying Monkey: A Theory of African-American Literary Criticism.* New York: Oxford University Press.

―――. 1993. "Beyond the Culture Wars: Identities in Dialogue." *Profession 93.* Modern Language Association, 1993. 6–11.

Gautier, Théophile. 1834. Preface to *Mademoiselle de Maupin* (1835). Reprint, New York: Modern Library, n.d.

George, Nelson. 1985. *Where Did Our Love Go? The Rise and Fall of the Motown Sound.* New York: St. Martin's.

―――. 1988. *The Death of Rhythm & Blues.* New York: Pantheon. Reprint, New York: Dutton, 1989.

Giddins, Gary. 1988. *Satchmo.* New York: Anchor.

―――. 1995. Conversation with Panama Francis.

Gillett, Charlie. 1970. *The Sound of the City: The Rise of Rock and Roll.* Revised ed. 1983. New York: Pantheon.

Gilroy, Paul. 1993. *The Black Atlantic: Modernity and Double Consciousness.* Cambridge: Harvard University Press.

Gitler, Ira. 1985. *Swing to Bop: An Oral History of the Transition in Jazz in the 1940s.* New York: Oxford University Press.

Goldrosen, John, and John Beecher. 1986. *Remembering Buddy: The Definitive Biography.* London: Pavilion. Reprint, New York: Penguin, 1987.

Gordy, Berry. 1994. *To Be Loved: The Music, the Magic, the Memories of Motown. An Autobiography.* New York: Warner Books.

Greene, Victor. 1992. *A Passion for Polka: Old-Time Ethnic Music in America.* Berkeley: University of California Press.

Grossman, James R., ed. 1994. Introduction to *The Frontier in American Cul-*

ture: An Exhibtion at the Newberry Library. Berkeley: University of California Press and the Newberry Library.

Guralnick, Peter. 1971. *Feel Like Going Home: Portraits in Blues & Rock 'n' Roll.* New York: Outerbridge & Dienstfrey. Reprint, New York: Vintage, 1981.

———. 1979. *Lost Highway: Journeys & Arrivals of American Musicians.* New York: Godine. Reprint, New York: Harper & Row, 1989.

———. 1986. *Sweet Soul Music: Rhythm and Blues and the Southern Dream of Freedom.* New York: Harper and Row.

Gurian, Jay. 1975. *Western American Writing: Tradition and Promise.* Deland, Fla.: Everett/Edwards.

Habermas, Jürgen. 1985. *The Philosophical Discourse of Modernity.* Translated by Frederick G. Lawrence. Cambridge: MIT Press, 1987.

Hamm, Charles. 1979. *Yesterdays: Popular Song in America.* New York: Norton.

Hammond, John, with Irving Townsend. 1977. *On Record: An Autobiography.* New York: Summit Books.

Hardy, Thomas. 1886. *The Mayor of Casterbridge.* Reprint, New York: Harper and Brothers, 1920.

Hebdige, Dick. 1979. *Subculture: The Meaning of Style.* London: Methuen.

Heyne, Eric, ed. 1992. *Desert, Garden, Margin, Range: Literature on the American Frontier.* New York: Twayne.

hooks, bell. 1996. *Bone Black: Memories of Girlhood.* New York: Henry Holt & Co.

Hughes, Langston. 1930. "Aesthete in Harlem." Reprinted in *The Collected Poems of Langston Hughes.* Edited by Arnold Rampersad. Co-edited by David Roessel. New York: Knopf, 1995.

Inman, Billie Andrew. 1981. *Walter Pater's Reading: A Bibliography of His Library Borrowings and Literary References, 1858–1873.* New York: Garland.

———. 1990. *Walter Pater and His Readings, 1874–1877, with a Bibliography of His Library Borrowings, 1878–1894.* New York: Garland.

Johnson, James Weldon. 1930. *Black Manhattan.* Reprint, New York: Da Capo, 1991.

Jones, LeRoi. 1963. *Blues People: Negro Music in White America.* New York: Morrow.

Jones, Max, and John Chilton. 1971. *Louis: The Louis Armstrong Story, 1900–1971.* Boston: Little, Brown.

Katz, William Loren. 1971. *The Black West.* Garden City: Doubleday. Third ed. 1987. Seattle: Open Hand. Reprint, New York: Touchstone, 1996.

Katznelson, Ira. 1973. *Black Men, White Cities: Race, Politics, and Migration in the United States, 1900–30, and Britain, 1948–68.* New York: Oxford University Press.

Keats, John. 1816. "On First Looking into Chapman's Homer." Reprinted in *Selected Poems and Letters*. Edited by Douglas Bush. Boston: Houghton Mifflin, 1959.

Keil, Charles. 1966. *Urban Blues*. Chicago: University of Chicago Press.

Kerouac, Jack. 1958. "The Essentials of Spontaneous Prose." *Evergreen Review* 2, no. 5 (summer): 72–73.

———. 1959. "Belief & Technique for Modern Prose." *Evergreen Review* 2, no. 8 (spring): 57.

Kolodny, Annette. 1984. *The Land Before Her: Fantasy and Experience of the American Frontiers, 1630–1860*. Chapel Hill: University of North Carolina Press.

Laing, R. D. 1967. *The Politics of Experience*. New York: Ballantine.

Lanham, Richard A. 1991. *A Handlist of Rhetorical Terms*. Second ed. Berkeley: University of California Press.

Lawlor, Mary. 1992. "The Fictions of Daniel Boone." In *Desert, Garden, Margin, Range: Literature on the American Frontier*. Edited by Eric Heyne. New York: Twayne.

Lawrence, D. H. 1921. *Psychoanalysis and the Unconscious*. Reprint, New York: Viking, 1962.

Leary, Timothy, et al. 1964. *Psychedelic Experience: A Manual Based on the Tibetan Book of the Dead*. Secaucus, N.J.: University Books.

Lee, Hermione. 1989. *Willa Cather: Double Lives*. New York: Pantheon. Reprint, New York: Vintage, 1991.

Lee, R. E. 1966. *From West to East*. Urbana: University of Illinois Press.

Lemann, Nicholas. 1991. *The Promised Land: The Great Black Migration and How It Changed America*. New York: Knopf. Reprint, New York: Vintage, 1992.

Levin, David, ed. 1975. *Emerson: Prophecy, Metamorphosis, and Influence: Selected Papers from the English Institute*. New York: Columbia University Press.

Levine, Lawrence W. 1977. *Black Culture and Black Consciousness: Afro-American Folk Thought from Slavery to Freedom*. New York: Oxford University Press.

Lewis, R. W. B. 1955. *The American Adam: Innocence and Tradition in the Nineteenth Century*. Chicago: University of Chicago Press.

Limerick, Patricia Nelson. 1987. *The Legacy of Conquest: The Unbroken Past of the American West*. New York: Norton.

Limerick, Patricia Nelson, et al., eds. 1991. *Trails: Toward a New Western History*. Lawrence: University of Kansas Press.

Mailer, Norman. 1957. *The White Negro*. Reprinted in *Advertisements for Myself* (1959). New York: G. P. Putnam's Sons. Reprint, New York: Berkley Medallion, 1966.

———. 1965. *An American Dream*. New York: Dial Press.

————. 1968. *The Armies of the Night: History as a Novel, the Novel as History*. New York: New American Library.

Malone, Bill C. 1985. *Country Music, U.S.A.* Austin: University of Texas Press.

Marcus, Greil. 1975. *Mystery Train: Images of America in Rock 'n' Roll Music*. New York: Dutton.

Marx, Leo. 1964. *The Machine in the Garden: Technology and the Pastoral Ideal in America*. New York: Oxford University Press.

Matthiessen, F. O. 1941. *American Renaissance: Art and Expression in the Age of Emerson and Whitman*. New York: Oxford University Press.

Meisel, Perry. 1976. "Joe Cocker Consults the Soul Doctors." *Village Voice*, 1 Mar. 89.

————. 1987. *The Myth of the Modern: A Study in British Literature and Criticism after 1850*. New Haven: Yale University Press.

Moers, Ellen. 1960. *The Dandy: Brummell to Beerbohm*. New York: Viking. Reprint, Lincoln: University of Nebraska Press, 1978.

Morgan, Thomas L., and William Barlow. 1992. *From Cakewalks to Concert Halls: An Illustrated History of African American Popular Music from 1895 to 1930*. Washington, D.C.: Elliott & Clark.

Morrison, Toni. 1987. *Beloved*. New York: Knopf. Reprint, New York: Plume, 1988.

Mumford, Lewis. 1926. *The Golden Day: A Study in American Experience and Culture*. New York: Boni and Liveright.

Murray, Albert. 1971. *South to a Very Old Place*. New York: McGraw-Hill. Reprint, New York: Vintage, 1991.

————. 1976. *Stomping the Blues*. New York: McGraw-Hill.

Nash, Gerald D., and Richard W. Etulain, eds. 1989. *The Twentieth-Century West: Historical Interpretations*. Albuquerque: University of New Mexico Press.

Nora, Pierre. 1992. Introduction to *Realms of Memory: The Construction of the French Past*. Vol. 2: *Traditions*. Translated by Arthur Goldhammer. New York: Columbia University Press, 1997.

————. 1994. "Between Memory and History: *Les Lieux de Mémoire*." Translated by Marc Roudebush. In *History & Memory in African-American Culture*. Edited by Geneviève Fabre and Robert O'Meally. New York: Oxford University Press.

Norman, Philip. 1996. *Rave On: The Biography of Buddy Holly*. New York: Simon and Schuster.

Palmer, Robert. 1981. *Deep Blues*. New York: Viking. Reprint, New York: Penguin, 1982.

————. 1992. "The Church of the Sonic Guitar." In *Present Tense: Rock & Roll Culture*. Edited by Anthony DeCurtis. Durham: Duke University Press.

Papanikolas, Zeese. 1995. *Trickster in the Land of Dreams*. Lincoln: University of Nebraska Press.

Pater, Walter. 1873. "Conclusion." *Studies in the History of the Renaissance*. Unless otherwise noted, all references from Pater's criticism are from *Selected Writings of Walter Pater*. Edited by Harold Bloom. New York: New American Library, 1974.

————. 1877. "The School of Giorgione." In *The Renaissance: Studies in Art and Poetry*.

————. 1885. *Marius the Epicurean*. Reprint, New York: Modern Library, n.d.

————. 1889. "Style." In *Appreciations*.

Pattison, Robert. 1987. *The Triumph of Vulgarity: Rock Music in the Mirror of Romanticism*. New York: Oxford University Press.

Pine, Richard. 1988. *The Dandy and the Herald: Manners, Mind, and Morals from Brummell to Durrell*. New York: St. Martin's.

Reed, Ishmael. 1969. *Yellow Back Radio Broke-Down*. Garden City: Doubleday. Reprint, New York: Avon, 1977.

————. 1972. *Mumbo Jumbo*. Garden City: Doubleday. Reprint, New York: Atheneum, n.d.

Robinson, Smokey, with David Ritz. 1989. *Smokey: Inside My Life*. New York: McGraw-Hill.

Rosenberg, Beth. 1995. *Virginia Woolf and Samuel Johnson: Common Readers*. New York: St. Martin's.

Russell, Don. 1978. Foreword to *The Life of Hon. William F. Cody, Known as Buffalo Bill, the Famous Hunter, Scout, and Guide: An Autobiography* (1879). Lincoln: University of Nebraska Press.

Russell, George. 1960. *The Lydian Chromatic Concept of Tonal Organization for Improvisation*. New York: Concept Publishing.

Russell, Ross. 1971. *Jazz Style in Kansas City and the Southwest*. Berkeley: University of California Press.

Said, Edward. 1978. *Orientalism*. New York: Pantheon.

Schuller, Gunther. 1989. *The Swing Era: The Development of Jazz, 1930–1945*. New York: Oxford University Press.

Seigel, Jerrold. 1986. *Bohemian Paris: Culture, Politics, and the Boundaries of Bourgeois Life, 1830–1930*. New York: Viking.

Shaw, Arnold. *Honkers and Shouters: The Golden Years of Rhythm and Blues*. New York: Macmillan. Reprint, New York: Collier Books, 1986.

Shelley, Percy Bysshe. 1816. "Mont Blanc." In *Selected Poetry*. Edited by Neville Rogers. Boston: Houghton Mifflin, 1968.

Simonson, Harold P. 1970. *The Closed Frontier: Studies in American Literary Tragedy*. New York: Holt, Rinehart and Winston.

————. 1983. *Radical Discontinuities: American Romanticism and Christian Consciousness*. London: Associated University Presses.

————. 1989. *Beyond the Frontier: Writers, Western Regionalism, and a Sense of Place.* Fort Worth: Texas Christian University Press.

Slotkin, Richard. 1973. *Regeneration Through Violence: The Mythology of the American Frontier.* Middletown: Wesleyan University Press.

————. 1985. *The Fatal Environment: The Myth of the Frontier in the Age of Industrialization, 1800–1890.* New York: Atheneum.

————. 1992. *Gunfighter Nation: The Myth of the Frontier in Twentieth-Century America.* New York: Atheneum.

Smith, Henry Nash. 1950. *Virgin Land: The American West as Symbol and Myth.* Cambridge: Harvard University Press. Reprint, New York: Vintage, n.d.

Southern, Eileen. 1971. *The Music of Black Americans: A History.* Second ed. 1983. New York: Norton.

Stearns, Marshall, and Jean Stearns. 1968. *Jazz Dance: The Story of American Vernacular Dance.* New York: Macmillan. Reprint, New York: Schirmer Books, 1979.

Stepto, Robert B. 1979. *From Behind the Veil: A Study of Afro-American Narrative.* Urbana: University of Illinois Press.

Sullivan, Jack. 1994. "New Worlds of Terror: The Legacy of Poe in Debussy and Ravel." *Literature, Interpretation, Theory* 5:83–93.

Tanner, Tony. 1965. *The Reign of Wonder: Naivety and Reality in American Literature.* Cambridge: Cambridge University Press.

Tompkins, Jane. 1992. *West of Everything: The Inner Life of Westerns.* New York: Oxford University Press.

Tosches, Nick. 1992. *Dino: Living High in the Dirty Business of Dreams.* New York: Doubleday.

Turner, Frederick Jackson. 1893. *The Frontier in American History.* Reprint, New York: Henry Holt, 1920.

Udall, Stuart L., ed. 1990. *Beyond the Mythic West.* Salt Lake City: Peregrine Smith Books.

Walker, Alice. 1970. "The Black Writer and the Southern Experience." Reprinted in *In Search of Our Mothers' Gardens: Womanist Prose.* New York: Harcourt, Brace & Co., 1983.

Walker, Don D. 1981. *Clio's Cowboys: Studies in the Historiography of the Cattle Trade.* Lincoln: University of Nebraska Press.

Washington, Booker T. 1901. *Up from Slavery: An Autobiography.* Reprint, New York: Carol, 1993.

Weisbuch, Robert. 1986. *Atlantic Double-Cross: American Literature and British Influence in the Age of Emerson.* Chicago: University of Chicago Press.

West, Cornel. 1989. *The American Evasion of Philosophy: A Genealogy of Pragmatism.* Madison: University of Wisconsin Press.

Wetmore, Helen Cody. 1899. *Last of the Great Scouts: The Life Story of*

Colonel William F. Cody, as Told by His Sister Helen Cody Wetmore. Reprint, Lincoln: University of Nebraska Press, 1965.

Wexler, Jerry, and David Ritz. 1993. *Rhythm and the Blues: A Life in American Music.* New York: Knopf.

White, G. Edward. 1968. *The Eastern Establishment and the Western Experience.* New Haven: Yale University Press.

Wilde, Oscar. 1879. "The Rise of Historical Criticism." In *Complete Writings of Oscar Wilde.* New York: Nottingham Society, 1909.

————. 1881. "The Grave of Shelley." In *The Works of Oscar Wilde.* New York: Brainard, 1909.

————. 1882a. "American Women." In *The Works of Oscar Wilde.* New York: Brainard, 1909.

————. 1882b. "American Lectures." In *The Works of Oscar Wilde.* New York: Brainard, 1909.

————. 1891. "The Decay of Lying." In *Intentions.* Reprinted in *The Artist as Critic: Critical Writings of Oscar Wilde.* Edited by Richard Ellmann. Chicago: University of Chicago Press, 1982.

Williams, Raymond. 1973. *The Country and the City.* New York: Oxford University Press.

Woolf, Virginia. 1919. "Modern Fiction." Reprinted in *Collected Essays.* New York: Harcourt, Brace & World, 1967.

————. 1925. *Mrs. Dalloway.* Reprint, New York: Harcourt, Brace & World, 1953.

————. 1928a. *Orlando.* Reprint, New York: Harcourt, Brace & Co., 1973.

————. 1928b. Introduction to *Mrs. Dalloway.* New York: Modern Library.

————. 1941. *Between the Acts.* Reprint, New York: Harcourt Brace Jovanovich, 1969.

Žižek, Slavoj. 1989. *The Sublime Object of Ideology.* London and New York: Verso.

Discography

Armstrong, Louis, and Ella Fitzgerald. 1956. *Ella and Louis.* Verve.

Baker, LaVern. 1956. "Jim Dandy" (Lincoln Chase). Atlantic.

Band, The. 1968. "I Shall Be Released" (Bob Dylan). *Music from Big Pink.* Capitol.

Beatles, The. 1965. *Rubber Soul.* Capitol. "Think for Yourself" (George Harrison); "I'm Looking Through You" and "Run for Your Life" (John Lennon/Paul McCartney).

————. 1966a. "Nowhere Man" (John Lennon/Paul McCartney). Capitol.

————. 1966b. *Revolver.* Capitol.

————. 1967. "With a Little Help from My Friends" (John Lennon/Paul McCartney). *Sgt. Pepper's Lonely Hearts Club Band.* Capitol.

Berry, Chuck. All recordings released by Chess.

Coasters, The. 1958. "Yakety Yak" (Jerry Leiber/Mike Stoller). Atco.

Curtis [Ousley], "King." 1964. "Soul Serenade" (Curtis Ousley/Luther Dixon). Capitol.

————. 1971. *King Curtis Live at Fillmore West*. Atco.

Davis, Miles. 1955. *Miles*. Prestige.

————. 1959. *Kind of Blue*. Columbia.

————. 1960. *Sketches of Spain*. Columbia.

————. 1963. *Seven Steps to Heaven*. Columbia.

————. 1968. *Miles in the Sky*. Columbia.

————. 1969. *In a Silent Way*. Columbia.

————. 1970. *Bitches Brew*. Columbia.

Dylan, Bob. 1964. *Another Side of Bob Dylan*. Columbia.

————. 1965a. *Bringing It All Back Home*. Columbia.

————. 1965b. *Highway 61 Revisited*. Columbia.

————. 1966. *Blonde on Blonde*. Columbia.

————. 1968. *John Wesley Harding*. Columbia.

————. 1970. *Self-Portrait*. Columbia.

Franklin, Aretha. 1968. "Seesaw" (Steve Cropper/Don Covay). *Aretha Now*. Atlantic.

Green, Al. 1972. All references are to *Let's Stay Together*. Hi. All songs by Al Green except "Let's Stay Together" (Willie Mitchell/Al Green/Al Jackson, Jr.), "I've Never Found a Girl" (Booker T. Jones, Jr./Eddie Floyd/Alvertis Isbell), and "How Can You Mend a Broken Heart?" (Barry Gibb/Robin Gibb).

[Hendrix, Jimi.] The Jimi Hendrix Experience. 1967. *Are You Experienced?* Reprise.

————. 1968a. *Axis: Bold as Love*. Reprise.

————. 1968b. *Electric Ladyland*. Reprise.

Hendrix, Jimi. 1970. *Band of Gypsys*. Capitol.

Holly, Buddy. 1962. "Reminiscing" (Curtis Ousley). Coral.

Led Zeppelin. 1969. "Whole Lotta Love" (Jimmy Page/Robert Plant/John Paul Jones/John Bonham/John Baldwin). *Led Zeppelin II*. Atlantic.

————. 1976. *Presence*. Atlantic.

Martha [Reeves] and the Vandellas. 1963. "Heat Wave" (Brian Holland/Lamont Dozier/Eddie Holland). Gordy.

Ramones, The. 1980. *End of the Century*. Sire.

[Robinson, Smokey, and] The Miracles. 1965a. "Ooo Baby Baby" (William Robinson, Jr./Warren Moore). Tamla.

————. 1965b. "The Tracks of My Tears" (William Robinson, Jr./Warren Moore/Marvin Tarplin). Tamla.

————. 1965c. "Going to a Go Go" (William Robinson, Jr./Warren Moore/Marvin Tarplin/Robert Rogers). Tamla.

Robinson, Smokey, and the Miracles. 1967. "I Second that Emotion" (William Robinson, Jr./Alfred Cleveland). Tamla.

Rolling Stones, The. 1966. "Paint It Black" (Mick Jagger/Keith Richards). London.

Waters, Muddy. All songs by McKinley Morganfield except "Southbound Train" (Bill Broonzy). All recordings released by Chess.

Wilson, Jackie. 1957. "Reet Petite" (Berry Gordy, Jr./Tyran Carlo). Brunswick.

———. 1958. "Lonely Teardrops" (Tyran Carlo/Berry Gordy, Jr./Gwendolyn Gordy). Brunswick.

———. 1959a. "That's Why (I Love You So)" (Tyran Carlo/Berry Gordy, Jr./Gwendolyn Gordy). Brunswick.

———. 1959b. "I'll Be Satisfied" (Tyran Carlo/Berry Gordy, Jr./Gwendolyn Gordy). Brunswick.

———. 1960. "A Woman, a Lover, a Friend" (Sidney J. Wyche). Brunswick.

———. 1961a. "Please Tell Me Why" (Paul Tarnopol). Brunswick.

———. 1961b. "You Don't Know What It Means" (Jackie Wilson/Alonzo Tucker/Morris Levy). Brunswick.

———. 1963. "Baby Workout" (Alonzo Tucker/Jackie Wilson). Brunswick.

———. 1965a. "Danny Boy" (Trad.). Brunswick.

———. 1965b. "No Pity (in the Naked City)" (Johnnie Roberts/Alonzo Tucker/Jackie Wilson). Brunswick.

INDEX